Jean Sutton Shauer

June 25. 14

Books by Joan Sutton

Lovers and Others. Toronto: Clarke Irwin & Co. Ltd., 1974.

Once More with Love. Toronto: Clarke Irwin & Co. Ltd., 1976.

Clothing and Culture. Toronto: McClelland & Stewart Limited, 1975.

Love Lines. Toronto: Toronto Sun Publishing, 1979.

All Men Are Not Alike. Toronto: McClelland & Stewart Limited, 1979.

A Legacy of Caring: The Society of Memorial Sloan-Kettering Cancer Center. Foreword by Laurence Rockefeller. New York: The Society of MSKCC, 1996.

To Diane who is the best

The
Alzheimer's
Diary

One woman's experience
from caregiver to widow

J O A N   S U T T O N

iUniverse LLC
Bloomington

THE ALZHEIMER'S DIARY
ONE WOMAN'S EXPERIENCE FROM CAREGIVER TO WIDOW

iUniverse books may be ordered through booksellers or by contacting:

iUniverse
1663 Liberty Drive
Bloomington, IN 47403
www.iuniverse.com
1-800-Authors (1-800-288-4677)

ISBN: 978-1-4917-3161-1 (sc)
ISBN: 978-1-4917-3162-8 (hc)
ISBN: 978-1-4917-3163-5 (e)

Library of Congress Control Number: 2014906588

Printed in the United States of America.

iUniverse rev. date: 05/02/2014

For my beloved Oscar

Even memory is not necessary for love. There is a land of the living and a land of the dead and the bridge is love.

—Thornton Wilder, *The Bridge of San Luis Rey* (1927)

Contents

Foreword xi

Preface xiii

Acknowledgements xvii

The Diagnosis 1

The Costs 4

A Treatment for Alzheimer's Disease? 7

Looking for a Cure 12

The Stealthy Thief 16

Memory, Past, Present and Future 19

Caregivers Unlimited 22

A Love Story 26

Know Thy Enemy 29

Advice Unlimited 33

One Caregiver's Philosophy 36

Tempering Temper 40

Caregiver Care 44

The Saints Among Us 47

Eight Steps to a Healthy Brain 50

Saving the Elderly 54

Old Folks Talking 57

The Rivers of My Memory 60

How Are You, Mom? 63

A Diverting Affair? 66

Why Know? 71

As Time Goes By.. 75

Death and Grieving... 79

Good-bye, My Love.. 80

Death: Getting to Know You.. 84

Comforting the Widowed... 87

Status: The Alzheimer's Widow 91

Grief: The Poor-Me Stage 94

The Mind-and-Body Connection... 98

The If-Onlys 101

The Not-So-Merry Widow.. 105

Anima 108

The Widow's Dower: Skin Hunger.. 111

Endless Love 114

Bibliography.. 117

Foreword

ALZHEIMER'S DISEASE AFFECTS US ALL.

Up to 40 percent of people who reach age 80 (that's most of us) will get Alzheimer's disease and suffer up to 10 years of progressive cognitive and functional decline, becoming increasingly dependent on others and ultimately entering a state in which the body remains but the mind is completely gone. This is an ungodly, surreal, zombie-like, humanoid state of being. Ultimately, everyone diagnosed will die from Alzheimer's disease, a chronic, progressive, inevitably fatal illness that kills mostly as a result of pneumonia that occurs when patients forget how to swallow, causing food to persistently get in the lungs.

Alzheimer's affects us all as friends and family, caregivers and supporters. Most of us will be caring for someone with Alzheimer's disease during our lifetime, perhaps a spouse, parent, sibling or friend.

And it is expensive. One year of home care or nursing home care costs about $100,000. Nationwide, Alzheimer's is the third most expensive disease after heart disease and cancer.

And now we think of Alzheimer's as a disease of young and middle age, not only because we now know that it begins in midlife as a result of new brain-scanning technology developed in part by our foundation, but also because the younger generations will bear the economic burden of the rapidly aging baby-boomer population that will suffer Alzheimer's disease.

But there is hope. Currently, more than 75 human clinical trials are testing new drugs for Alzheimer's disease. Our foundation, the Alzheimer's Drug Discovery Foundation (www.AlzDiscovery.org), has received over 3,000 new ideas for new drugs for Alzheimer's since 1998, and we have funded over 420 of these in 18 countries. The FDA approved the first diagnostic test for Alzheimer's disease in 2012, a test also developed by our foundation. Collaborative efforts of foundations like ours, government (the National Institutes of Health), industry (pharmaceutical and biotechnology companies) and academic institutions are all working together to discover new drugs.

In the meantime, the suffering of patients and their caregivers remains paramount. Their struggles and triumphs are the real story of Alzheimer's disease. Joan Sutton Straus knows this reality personally and deeply. That is certainly clear from her passionate, sometimes desperate, sometimes humorous and always honest and forthright story of her life with her beloved husband as he declined into the depths.

Sharing stories of our lives brings us together. Joan does that so well.

Howard Fillit, MD
The Alzheimer's Drug Discovery Foundation

Preface

My husband and I had been together for 26 years when, in 2006, he was diagnosed with Alzheimer's disease (AD).

Seven years later, I observed our wedding anniversary as a widow.

For me, the intervening years were a roller coaster of emotions as I assumed new responsibilities, learned new skills and lived with an aching loneliness of the heart. Although my husband could not communicate his feelings as he passed through the various stages of Alzheimer's, I am certain he experienced great frustration, embarrassment, anger, fear—all the emotions one would expect when a proud and productive man finds himself being robbed of dignity and self. But then, I firmly believe that even in the worst stages of Alzheimer's, there is a human being in there, lost but still present.

Writing has always been therapy for me, and these essays began as a way for me to sort out my own emotions and express my frustration at the lack of curative treatment as well as my fury at the gods for letting this happen to my beloved partner. As I had been a journalist, writing a daily column for the *Toronto Sun* and then the *Toronto Star,* friends suggested that I post my thoughts as a blog on

WordPress.com. I hesitated. It is one thing to write about myself but it was quite another to discuss my husband's illness in public.

As I began to learn more about AD, I recognized the need for public pressure to support more research. In speaking out, I was encouraged by the examples of Nancy Reagan, Yasmin Khan (whom I interviewed for the *Toronto Star* about the effects of Alzheimer's on her mother, Rita Hayworth), Glen Campbell, the family of the legendary New York Giants running back Ron Johnson, and, Mel Goodes, the former CEO of Warner-Lambert.

Mel became a vocal advocate for Alzheimer's patients when he was diagnosed, at the age of 74, with AD. His words about trying to find relevance "in a world where Alzheimer patients are not supposed to be seen or heard" rang a bell with me. I too needed to find some relevance, some way to make sense of what was happening to my husband, to me, and to our family. That led to my accepting Leonard Lauder's invitation to join the board of overseers of the Alzheimer's Drug Discovery Foundation and my decision to publish my essays. Shortly after starting with *WordPress,* Danielle Crittenden Frum asked me to join the *Huffington Post.* Most of the essays in this book have been published in those forums. Where necessary, I have updated them, and in some cases, I have provided new information. I wrote them as stand-alone pieces, some of which would be of more interest to readers than others, so some basic information is repeated.

Not being of the Internet generation, I wasn't sure what a blog was (and didn't like the sound of the word—*essay* sounds so much more dignified), but I gave it a try, not sure anyone out in that strange universe would be interested. To my surprise, there was a response—although the *Huffington Post* does not keep statistics for bloggers, *WordPress.com* has recorded more than 5,000 views from 40 countries around the world. That is gratifying to me as a writer, but it is also sobering, as the number reflects another set of numbers—the terrifying statistics of those who have or are affected by Alzheimer's disease.

I learned many things on this journey—not only about the disease but also about my family, my friends and myself. It is common to use *battle* or *fight* as a metaphor when describing reactions to a disease. In my battle with Alzheimer's, love was my armor. I cannot begin to repay the many people who accompanied me through these years.

My Bellport, Long Island, neighbours were great sources of strength. Annie Rohrmeier gave me a Scotch, a shoulder, and permission to cry; Roy Eddey and Dr. Joel Hershey provided spontaneous gestures of friendship; and Joel, dear Joel, was with us during the final moments of my husband's life. Dr. Philip Stieg spent Saturday afternoons sharing a cigar and that special male silence with my beloved and Dennis Borro was my philosopher king. Dr. Richard Berman gave tender care to my husband all through our Long Island years and, with his wife, Chantal, was among the many who made places in their social lives for a man who was increasingly absent. Others who did that so generously include Pat and Steve Gross, Jackie and Tom Latimer, Rick and Sue Salomon, Robin and Pete Roe, Dr. Leon Root and his dear wife, Paula, Duane Elliott, who made this sad journey before me, and my friend Shirley Maytag King, who walked more than 20 blocks in the aftermath of Hurricane Sandy to make sure we were all right. (We were stranded on the 46th floor without elevators, electricity or water for two days.) When the family lawyer is not just a legal advisor, but friend and advocate, as Pete Roe has been to me, it is a blessing to a caregiver struggling with major decisions.

My husband had a great capacity for friendship. He was loyal to his friends, who encompassed all ages and all sorts, and they were faithful to him. In the last years, several of the young men he'd mentored were regular companions to him—Chuck Locke and Percy Preston shared many a struggling conversation with him at the Knickerbocker Club. We could not have managed the last year without the help of Oscar Straus Schafer.

Thank you.

We were fortunate to have such friends and fortunate too in the medical care available, including that provided by Dr. Veronica Lo Fasso and Deirdre Mole at the Irving Wright Center of New York Hospital and Dr. Julia Fahey and the staff of the Brookhaven Medical Center Hospice. Dr. Simon McGrail monitored care from his home in Halifax, Nova Scotia, always ready to help me navigate conflicting opinions. Martha Murch and Gene Cruz were much more than aides—they were with me for the last two years of my husband's illness and his death. I will never forget their dedication, and I cherish their friendship.

Of family, I cannot say enough. They brought love, honour and respect to my husband, especially in the last difficult year, and I took refuge in their understanding. I am particularly grateful to my children, Deborah and Walter, and Mark Robie, who helped in practical as well as emotional ways. Somehow, in the midst of the worst days, we found the healing magic of laughter. My husband would have approved of that—he loved to laugh.

It is my hope that anyone struggling with the impact of Alzheimer's disease will find something helpful in these essays, that those who have been diagnosed with Alzheimer's will be encouraged to take part in clinical trials and, above all, that readers will speak out about the need for more research, more geriatric specialists and more assistance to families caring for their loved ones at home.

Acknowledgements

I WOULD LIKE TO THANK DR. HOWARD FILLIT, EXECUTIVE
director and chief science officer of the Alzheimer's Drug Discovery
Foundation, for sharing his knowledge and vetting the scientific
and medical facts in these essays; the Alzheimer's Drug Discovery
Foundation for permission to quote from their website advice on
how to achieve and maintain cognitive vitality with aging; and
especially, Ronald and Leonard Lauder for establishing this non-
profit organization, with its important mission: to accelerate the
discovery of drugs to prevent, treat and cure Alzheimer's disease,
related dementias and cognitive aging.

This book is all the better because of the careful reading and
suggestions of Kathy Brooks, John Millyard and Phebe Port

All profits from the sale of this book will benefit ADDF/
Canada.

The
Alzheimer's
Diary

The Diagnosis

ALZHEIMER'S. GIVEN THAT WE WERE IN THE NEUROLOGIST'S office at my request, I should not have been surprised—no, not surprised, but floored, shocked! —by the diagnosis. But I was.

That visit to the doctor was the result of a cluster of seemingly small incidents. First, my husband was just about to go out the door when I noticed that he was wearing one black shoe and one brown one. I thought, *Well, if the closet is not well lit, anyone can make that mistake,* so it was not a major concern. However, as he had the elegance of Fred Astaire, a fair degree of vanity and managed to look like a fashion plate even in fishing clothes, it was a bit troubling. But we laughed and made a joke of it, and he changed to a matching pair.

The next incident was more worrisome. When we were home I made breakfast and dinner, he prepared lunch. But one day, there was no lunch and, when I asked if we were going out to eat, he replied that he had already eaten, that he'd had lunch with John L. As John L. had been dead for several years, I was thrown, but I didn't say anything—I just made sandwiches for both of us. He ate his and, later in the day, came to me and said, "I think I did something foolish earlier today." I hugged him and told him that it was not foolish to think so vividly of a beloved friend.

After that, I was more watchful.

Then the phone rang—it was the bank, advising me that we had a considerable overdraft. That was so unlike my Princeton economics–educated husband that it was clear something was very wrong.

Soon we were at the neurologist's office, where the doctor ordered a battery of tests. I was in the room with him when he took the cognitive ones, and I realized for the first time how dependent he had become on me. When asked a question, he looked to me for the answer. The doctor suggested that I sit behind him. When challenged to alphabetically list four-legged animals, he got to *F* and then came up not with a four-legged animal but a four-letter word. That was the beginning of his many attempts in the coming years to turn the subject away from what he could not do with a caustic remark or humour. Blood work and various scans followed the cognitive tests, and then I found myself standing in the doctor's office, hearing those words: "early dementia, first-stage Alzheimer's—AD."

I didn't believe it. I had a picture in my mind of the Alzheimer's patient—looking angry and untidy, struggling to feed him- or herself, not recognizing people, wandering off mindlessly. My husband was not like that—not anything like that. Yes, there were troubling incidents, but he was getting older—surely his behaviour was just due to aging. And if not aging, then perhaps he'd had a small stroke or there was some manageable "Take this pill, and it will all go away" treatment. *Please*!

I failed to recognize that my mental portrait of the Alzheimer's patient was of someone in the end stages. The first stages of the disease do not look anything like that, there are no visual clues. And so I began the doctor search. One, two, three—all concurred. And all the while, my husband was becoming more and more tired of the routine—dressing, undressing, being poked and prodded and asked to memorize, to remember several different items, to draw a clock.

At last, I faced the fact that I was doing this not for him but for myself. I wanted the answer to be different. Clearly, it would not be. Like it or not—and I didn't—I had to accept the truth. And so my beloved husband became one of the 5 million Americans and 3 million Canadians diagnosed with this thief of a disease.

One of the first things I learned was that the recorded number of those afflicted is grossly inaccurate. That's only North America—the numbers affected worldwide are formidable. And even those statistics are deceiving, because for every individual diagnosed, a circle of others—partners, family, friends, employers and employees—are also victims, robbed of memory and relationships. Society now recognizes the caregivers and the heavy burden they bear. But others also pay the emotional, physical and financial prices: children who become parents to their parents, grandchildren deprived of that special relationship, partners who see years of intimacy vanish as if they never were. And society itself, robbed of all that brain power and burdened by the cost of care.

And so, in 1996, I began my seven-year journey, the passage of time that Nancy Reagan described as "the long good-bye."

The Costs

In 2006, THREE NEUROLOGISTS AGREED: MY HUSBAND HAD early Alzheimer's (AD).

He was a man of innate elegance and dignity and was a private person—so private that I hesitated to share personal matters with an impersonal public. But Alzheimer's does not recognize elegance, dignity or privacy. It is the one-size-fits-all disease: whether you pump gas at the local station or sit in the back of a limo, walk the Fifth Avenue beat or look down on the park from your penthouse, whether you are a rocket scientist or a rock and roller, fit or flabby, Alzheimer's makes no distinction.

Yet even though millions of people have the disease, there is still something of a stigma about the label. Just as cancer used to be a diagnosis whispered in close family circles, despite the numbers, many react the same way to Alzheimer's. People picture the crazy aunt or uncle locked away in the attic. The first reaction to the diagnosis is often, like mine, denial.

Even when someone dies, there can be denial. Instead of writing that someone has died of Alzheimer's or complications of AD, in many obituaries families list the cause of death as pneumonia or some other infection. Yet those infections are almost always the result of AD. For example, in the later stages of AD, the patient will have difficulty swallowing. As a result, he or she inhales food, and that can lead to pneumonia. The patient does indeed die of pneumonia—but AD was the cause of the pneumonia. The patient died from complications of Alzheimer's disease. We should not soften that fact.

That is why I admire Mel Goodes. Canadian born, Queen's University educated, Mel was diagnosed with Alzheimer's a few years ago. For several years, he spoke about his diagnosis at Alzheimer Drug Discovery Foundation events. Looking at him, listening to him at those symposia, we saw, not the stereotype of the Alzheimer patient, but a man in the prime of his life, with a family who loved him, a man condemned to an ever narrowing future. It was hard to believe that he had Alzheimer's. Now, the disease has staked its claim and Mel is no longer able to speak at the ADDF events. If the Goodes family can take that public scrutiny as the disease progresses, so can our family. Everyone AD touches needs to speak out—public pressure is necessary if we are to find a more effective treatment or cure for this thief called Alzheimer's.

Alzheimer's affects 8 million North Americans now, with triple that number a probability when the baby boomers become senior citizens. The drug companies can tell us the cost of bringing a drug to market, but how do we measure the cost of not bringing a drug to market? In 2012, Alzheimer's cost the US economy $200 billion. In the December 2013 issue of the *AARP Bulletin,*[1] Senator Susan Collins pointed out that of that $200 billion, "$142 billion is from Medicare and Medicaid—and yet we invest a measly $500 million in research into Alzheimer's. That doesn't make sense."

---

1   http://ww.aarp.org/bulletin.

As to the personal cost, make no mistake: Alzheimer's might be a disease of the brain, but it is paid for with the currency of the heart—the child who will never know the special bond with a grandparent; sons and daughters who, at the height of their careers, are asked to take on responsibility for their parents; caregivers who give up their lives before their patients do; partners, whose days and nights are filled with an aching loneliness of the heart.

Over the past few years, in the middle of the night, I have found myself remembering the second verse of Francis William Bourdillon's poem:

> The mind has a thousand eyes,
> And the heart but one;
> Yet the light of a whole life
> Dies when love is done.

Only I rewrite the last line to read as follows:

> The light of a whole life dies
> When Alzheimer's comes.

Because, although the disease brings in its wake exhaustion and financial stress, the worst, the very worst, is being forced to watch the light that animates a human being go out bit by bit in someone you love.

That experience brings with it an overwhelming sense of hopelessness, because so far, there is no cure for Alzheimer's.

There are no survivors.

A Treatment for Alzheimer's Disease?

THERE IS NO DRUG ON THE MARKET THAT WILL STOP Alzheimer's from progressing.

There is no cure.

No one who has Alzheimer's will survive.

These are bald, brutal statements, but they are the truth.

That doesn't mean we should write the patients off. The patient can and should be treated. There are drugs that can help lessen symptoms for a limited time, and there are medications available that will make the patient more comfortable and make life a little easier for the caregiver—again, for a limited time.

But no matter how wealthy you are, whom you know, where you are, what hospital you visit, which city you live in, whom your doctor is or how energetic you are about your research, nothing will alter the fact that, at the moment, there is no proven effective treatment, no cure and no recovery from Alzheimer's. The journey from diagnosis to death can take up to 20 years—years during which families must deal with emotional and financial stress as well as caregiver exhaustion.

The taxpayer also shares the burden. Care for Alzheimer's patients in the United States now costs $200 billion a year and some believe that when the baby boomers reach senior status, the spiralling cost to the economy will break the health-care systems in both the United States and Canada. If research money were allocated according to the burden imposed on individuals and taxpayers, Alzheimer's would be near the top of the list, if not at the top. But research money is not allocated according to need or burden. In a National Institutes of Health (NIH) paper entitled "Funding Levels and Burden of Disease" published on February 24, 2011, the writer notes, "It is unclear why particular conditions remain under- or over-funded, relative to disease burden."

The writer lists strong political influence, charity revenue that leads to group advocacy, lobbying, private resources and the priorities of elected officials as some of the factors that influence funding choices. The money made available to breast cancer research and AIDS is a good example of how effective political pressure and public awareness can be. Nancy Reagan; Rita Hayworth's daughter, Princess Yasmin Khan; the Ron Johnson family; the Lauder family; Glen Campbell; Mel Goodes; the Alzheimer's Association; and the Alzheimer's Drug Discovery Foundation are among the voices urging more research into Alzheimer's. Every Alzheimer's family needs to join them in speaking out, insisting: attention must be paid.

Given the millions of people affected and the epidemic that will result from the baby boomers coming to Alzheimer's age, one must ask why the pharmaceutical companies, with all their expertise, have not developed better drugs to treat a guaranteed market. Part of the answer lies in economics. *Forbes* magazine (August 15, 2013) estimated that it costs more than $6 billion to bring a drug to market, and to make the economic picture even worse, 95 percent of experimental meds fail.

I suspect there is a certain amount of ageism at work as well. The popular view of Alzheimer's is that it is an old person's disease, and the thought that follows that might be *Old people are going to die anyway, so why put resources into that?* Age is indeed a major factor in contracting Alzheimer's, but not everyone who gets the disease is old, and even those who are old surely deserve a better ending.

There are drugs on the market that, while they do not treat the disease, may alleviate some of the symptoms. In a report updated in July 2012, ConsumerReports.org estimated the cost of Alzheimer drugs to be between $177 and $400 a month.

When my husband was diagnosed in 2006, There were two drugs that might slow the progress of the disease. My husband started taking one, Aricept, and as his progress through the various stages was slow, I have to assume that it had some effect. When the second drug was added to his treatment plan, he became so agitated and distressed that our doctor eliminated it from the protocol. When he first started on Aricept, it cost $600 for a three-month supply in the United States. Even if someone could afford it, that was a lot to pay for something that might or might not work. Certainly it was priced way beyond what most families could afford to spend. Eventually, a generic version came on the market, making it more accessible.

Today there are three drugs commonly prescribed in the early stages of AD. One of them, Aricept, has also been approved by the FDA for treatment of moderate to severe Alzheimer's, along with Namemba.

What is in the pipeline?

In its 2011–2012 Alzheimer's Disease Progress Report, the National Institutes of Health listed three areas of research: reducing beta-amyloid, targeting tau, and supporting neurogenesis. For more detailed information on these, I suggest readers consult the NIH National Institute on Aging's Alzheimer's Disease Education and Referral Center (www.nia.nih.gov/alzheimers). You can also find details about clinical trials on that NIH website, as well as from the Alzheimer's Association or the neurology department of your local hospital. However, as important as these trials are, they do not offer quick solutions. It takes from 10 to 15 years for a drug to pass through all the necessary testing before it is deemed safe enough for distribution to the public.

The Alzheimer's Drug Discovery Foundation, founded by Ronald and Leonard Lauder, is one of the largest sources of private funding for Alzheimer's research. Founded as a public charity in 2004, ADDF has one focussed goal: to develop drugs that will provide more effective treatment for Alzheimer's and lead to prevention or a cure within the next ten years. Since its founding, ADDF has provided $60 million in funding to 400 programs in 18 countries. The emphasis of its scientific committee, headed by Dr. Howard Fillit, is research into repurposing existing drugs as potential Alzheimer's treatments.

The story of Viagra provides one of the most dramatic examples of how a drug created for one thing can have a benefit in another area. Viagra began as a drug tested for angina, a heart condition that constricts the vessels that supply blood to the heart. The drug wasn't successful for that purpose, and the company— Pfizer—was about to withdraw it, when patients started to report a significant side effect: the men in the trial were having erections. Needless to say, Viagra is now a much-prescribed and highly profitable medication.

So is there an Alzheimer's Viagra? Eight million families hope that is the case. As useful as support groups, information booklets and other resources might be, as a caregiver, what I wanted more than anything was a drug that would alter the course of the disease.

Looking for a Cure

ONE OF THE BEST SOURCES FOR INFORMATION ABOUT Alzheimer's, from cause to potential cures, is the National Institutes of Health website, (http://www.nia.nih.gov/alzheiemrs). As I am on the board of overseers of the Alzheimer's Drug Discovery Foundation, (ADDF), I also closely follow its funding decisions (http://www.alzdisovery.org).

ADDF's scientific effort today emphasizes the potential in repurposing drugs already on the market. A promising project in clinical trials explores the glucose-insulin needs of the brain. Several years ago, Dr. Suzanne Craft of the University of Washington and Veterans Affairs, Puget Sound, approached ADDF to request funding for an idea that Dr. Howard Fillit, executive director and chief science officer of ADDF, says "seemed risky at the time." Dr. Craft believed that people with Alzheimer's should be given insulin, delivered through a nasal spray.

Explaining the science behind the initiative, Dr. Fillit points out that although the brain represents only 3 percent of the body weight, it uses 25 percent of the oxygen and glucose we consume, for energy purposes. As Dr. Fillit notes, "The brain is extremely metabolically active compared to other organs and very dependent on oxygen and glucose. In order to change glucose into energy, the brain has to have insulin."

He adds, "There has always been a theory that Alzheimer's begins with the aging of a part of the cells that creates energy, called mitochondria. With aging, mitochondria become less efficient." He explains, "While most organs can replenish themselves—in the liver, when cells die, new cells are born—in the brain, we lay down circuits early in life and the majority of those circuits don't change. The cells in our brain are as old as we are; they are constantly being ravaged.

"Dr. Craft's idea is that—because insulin enables cells to use glucose more efficiently—we should be giving AD patients insulin to the brain. But you can't give non-diabetic people insulin systemically because they would become hypoglycemic. She thought that if we could deliver insulin through the nose it would go directly to the brain the same way that cocaine goes directly to the brain, without harmful changes to blood insulin or glucose levels throughout the body. We funded her about eight years ago to create an intranasal delivery system to a pilot study group, to see what would happen to their cognitive function."

The participants were diagnosed with mild to moderate AD or mild cognitive impairment (MCI). Their memory, cognition and ability to function were measured before and after the four-month trial period. "And," says Dr. Fillit, "guess what? Their cognitive function improved and that is unusual. If you look at a lot of the clinical trials, sometimes you will get an outcome on biomarkers, but rarely do you get an outcome for cognitive function."[2]

As a result of initial ADDF funding, Dr. Craft's pilot program has received follow-on funding from the NIH's Institute on Aging

---

2   Dr. Howard Fillit interview with the author, New York, 2013.

and the US Department of Veterans Affairs. Last year, it was one of three projects selected by the NIH to receive $7.9 million of the funding made available by President Obama's National Plan to Address Alzheimer's Disease. For the past year, Dr. Craft and her team have been conducting treatment trials at multiple sites across the United States. The hope is that this insulin spray will have both an immediate effect—the brain lights up right away—and a long-term one whereby the insulin contribution will protect cells from dying.

At the Alzheimer's Association International Conference 2013, held in Boston, Dr. Craft reported "long-acting intranasal insulin imparted a significant memory boost to patients with mild cognitive impairment of Alzheimer's disease who carried a high risk allele for the disease." More study is under way with a one-year program called SNIFF. This will include 240 subjects who will receive insulin or a placebo. Researchers will assess tests of cognition and memory and changes in daily functioning at various periods during the study.

Another potential drug repurposing is in clinical trials at the Toronto Dementia Research Alliance at the University of Toronto. ADDF, in collaboration with the W. Garfield Weston Foundation, recently announced funding to support a clinical trial investigating the potential for hypertension drugs to slow Alzheimer's disease progression. Dr. Sandra Black, who holds the Brill Chair in neurology at the Department of Medicine, University of Toronto, and is the director of research for the Brain Sciences Program at Sunnybrook Health Services Center in Toronto, is leading the study. Announcing the grant, Dr. Fillit explained, "Hypertension has been suggested to be a risk factor for Alzheimer's disease for almost 30 years, yet we have not adequately translated this knowledge into the clinic for the benefit of patients. Dr. Black's study will begin to address this important issue in a novel study design, investigating the possibility that some anti-hypertensive agents may also be neuroprotective."

Once, Alzheimer's was considered to be such a hopeless diagnosis that no one wanted to put money or scientific effort into drug discovery. Now, thanks to President Obama's National Plan to Address Alzheimer's Disease and people like the Lauders, Dr. Fillit and others in the field, that has changed. Getting a drug to market is a long, expensive and risky venture but it is happening and that is good news for Alzheimer's patients and their families. They know, too well, the cost of not bringing more effective drugs to the market—to caregivers, patients and everyone who loves them.

The Stealthy Thief

I HAVE COME TO THINK OF ALZHEIMER'S DISEASE AS A CAT burglar—a stealthy thief with infinite patience. He doesn't steal all your memory at once—he just slips in and takes a little bit here and a little bit there and then disappears for a while. You start to think you are safe. But back he comes, to take another piece of the precious self—and all that goes with it.

At the outset, the neurologists explained to me that my husband was in the early stage of Alzheimer's. This, by the way, should not be confused with early-onset Alzheimer's. The latter is a fairly rare type that attacks people under the age of 65.

Two doctors told me he had lost "executive function," which sounded to me like gobbledygook doctor-speak—my husband was not in the running to become the CEO of a company. But the third doctor explained the situation better. He said that my husband had lost "the memory of procedure."

That explained why he could no longer write a cheque or balance the chequebook. *Well, that's not so bad. I can do that,* I thought. After all, I had handled my own finances before our marriage. This situation was a little more complicated and somewhat delicate. But it was doable and not the end of the world—for me.

But I wondered, *What about him?* And I asked myself, not for the last time, "What, if anything, does my husband know, think about this?" He had been in charge of our finances, spent time every day at his desk, read the business pages, and managed his own investments. Was he aware that he was no longer capable of these responsibilities? Did it bother him? Did he hate losing this control? He saw me with the chequebook, and he said nothing. I wondered, *In taking over, am I hurting his feelings? Diminishing him? How do I navigate in this world of Alzheimer's?*

This definition also explained what had taken place in the kitchen. My husband had always been passionate about food. When we first married, I would do all the shopping and meal planning during the week, thinking that such a busy man shouldn't have to worry about groceries on the weekend. Wrong—he wanted to be in the fish market, in the cheese store, at the vegetable stand. Over the years, food became a large part of our marriage. We planned menus together, shopped together, cooked together, critiqued together and tasted food and wine together. It was more than cooking—it was fun and laughter; it was sensual.

Now this man who'd prepared a perfect rack of lamb persillé (carving it in the French manner), whipped up a cheese soufflé (his whisk beating out a samba), never used a bottle dressing and browned adroitly the crust on the crème brûlée stood looking at the bread, lettuce, meat and mustard and did not know what to do. He could not assemble a sandwich.

His face showed frustration, anger, and then embarrassment. He walked away, saying he was not hungry. I vowed that I would never let him be in a position again where he was face to face with something he could not do. I would be the protector of his dignity.

But that became a delicate dance, as I balanced encouraging him to participate against the possibility of him believing that he had failed. His limitations were not failures—the word failure was not in our vocabulary.

Of course, I could do all the cooking—that would not be a hardship. Millions of partners just assume that they will do it. But it was not the need to take on that task that angered me. It was the loss of what that meant to us. A large part of our days revolved around food. What would fill that time now? At first, I tried to involve him. When I was making a stew, I asked him to sit in the kitchen with me, where I gave him the task of cutting the meat into small pieces. He stayed with it for a few minutes and then, again, walked away. This part of our life together was clearly over.

Alzheimer's had now stolen two pieces of my husband's self—his ability to manage his finances and his joy in cooking—and, with those, a large part of his dignity. And this thief had robbed me too—of companionship, laughter and what our friends used to call our ballet in the kitchen.

Something like this happens when Alzheimer's becomes part of any relationship. Whether it is golf, gardening, backyard barbecues or fights over the remote, Alzheimer's steals something precious—not just from one life but from two.

Memory, Past, Present and Future

WHEN WE HAVE MEMORY, WE TAKE IT FOR GRANTED. Six years ago, if I thought about memory at all, it was as a photograph album, a sentimental depository of the past where we preserve the faces of those we love and why we love them, the rites of passage—ours and others'—and our successes, failures and lessons learned. All of these combine to form a tapestry that defines who we are. Our pasts are important. Who are we if we lose them?

But memory is not just our past—it is also our present. Memory tells us how to send an e-mail, get from here to there, to put on our underpants before our outerwear, how to use a knife and fork and even swallow. Memory is the *on* button for every function we take for granted.

However, memory defines not only our past and present but also our future. Without memory, instead of growing older as a rational, aware, independent person, we will become one of the millions cared for, dependent on others to make our decisions and monitor our every function. I think we would hate ending our lives that way, but would we know? Would we realize what was happening to us?

That is the mystery that surrounds all Alzheimer's patients: How much are they aware of what they are losing? There were days when I thought my husband had disappeared mentally, just gone, so there was no point in considering him when making a decision. And then, suddenly, he was back, bright, aware. Those moments were few, and they didn't last long, but they were bright with hope—false hope perhaps, but hope.

When AD patients get angry, as many do, is it anger directed at themselves and prompted by the fact that—just as a stroke victim struggles for words that are there but won't come out—perhaps the Alzheimer patient is infuriated by a nagging awareness that there is something he or she should be doing but cannot remember what or how?

We all worry when we can't find our keys or our chequebooks. We tease ourselves with the diagnosis of having old-timer's disease. But the challenges of Alzheimer's disease are different. It is not a matter of being able to find the chequebook—it's remembering how to write a cheque. With my husband's diagnosis of Alzheimer's and the explanation that he had lost the memory of procedure, I realized that memory can be segmented.

Individuals with Alzheimer's might remember faces but forget how to make a sandwich; they might stand up when a woman enters the room but forget the name of the president. And the progress of Alzheimer's through its various stages can be confusing because moments of clarity can be mixed in with the dementia.

Many websites describe the stages of Alzheimer's, but Alzheimer's patients are still individuals. To paraphrase Abraham Lincoln, who, when speaking about the ability to fool people, is quoted as saying, "You can fool some of the people all of the time and all of the people some of the time, but you can't fool all of the people all of the time," Alzheimer's patients might have some of the symptoms all of the time and all of the symptoms some of the time, but it is unlikely that all patients will have all the symptoms all of the time.

I must point out that I am not a doctor, neurologist, nurse or scientist. What I describe are my own observations based on a small sample group—my husband and a friend's husband, who was two years older than mine and two years beyond mine in staging. These men shared similar backgrounds and education, the same neurologist and the same diagnosis, and his wife was, as I was, determined to keep her husband at home. As alike as our husbands were, they were not alike in the way the disease affected them. To this narrow perspective, I add years of reading message boards, articles and books.

My experience and research have led me to conclude that there is a human trinity: the brain, the mind and what some might call the soul but I call the essence—the anima—of a being. I think of the brain as a machine. Parts of it wear out and break down, but even as that is happening, the mind can still be there and can spring seemingly out of nowhere to the forefront. From time to time, even the blankest of eyes will shine with soul. This is the yo-yo motion of the progress of Alzheimer's as I have witnessed it. Every once in a while, someone, that unique human being, is still present.

And that was why I was convinced that the soul—the essence, the anima—of the one I loved would be there until the end.

Caregivers Unlimited

I AM ALWAYS SURPRISED WHEN SOMEONE REFERS TO ME AS A caregiver. I don't think of myself in those terms—I am a wife honouring the vows I took so many years ago.

I have had the better and the richer, and here, I am speaking of experiences, not money.

Now I am living through their opposites: the sickness and the poorer but, in this case, I am speaking of both experiences and money, because Alzheimer's is expensive. Round-the-clock home care in an urban centre can cost $120,000 a year. Nursing-home costs vary, but a range between $75,000 and $100,000 a year is fairly typical. Who pays these costs—government, insurance or the family—varies from individual to individual, state to state and country to country. Researching what resources are available is an important part of the Alzheimer's learning curve.

There are probably many partners who, like me, just step up to bat without adding the title of caregiver to their names. This is why, perhaps, according to Paula Span's article "New Numbers on Elder Care,"[3] the majority of the 39.8 million respondents to a survey identified themselves as unpaid caregivers to parents or grandparents, while only 4 percent said they were caring for a spouse or partner.

There are many more of us than that. We just don't call it caregiving. We are, quite simply, doing our duty.

Ah, duty. Louisa May Alcott wrote a poem on that subject that reads as follows:

> I slept, and dreamed that life was beauty,
> I woke and found that life is duty.

Duty—it sounds like a harsh word, rather mean, a bare-bones approach to responsibility. Yet there can be beauty in the duty. That marriage of duty and beauty is captured in the other version of this thought, this one written by the Indian poet Rabindranath Tagore:

> I slept and dreamt that life was joy. I awoke and saw
> that life was service.
> I acted and behold, service was joy.

However we define duty, where there is an Alzheimer's patient, there is a caregiver, and we are a diverse lot, we partners in this Alzheimer's world.

There are those who wrap themselves in duty, taking from it a whole new definition of self. For many, the act of taking care of someone gives their lives meaning beyond anything experienced before. There are others, at the opposite extreme, who cannot meet the demands. And many, like me, who muddle along, doing what we can at any given time.

---

3   Paula Span, "New Numbers on Elder Care," *New York Times*, July 5, 2012.

We have created the corollary to the Alzheimer's world: the caregivers' world. We turn to each other in support groups at community centres or online to share insights, practical tips, despair and encouragement. For me, the Internet message boards were invaluable. I found the *New York Times* blog *The New Old Age*, with its broad approach and contributions by various writers and professionals, a great source of information.

When I wanted to connect with others who are in my situation, I turned to *The Alzheimer's Reading Room.* (htttp://www.alzheimersreadingroom.org). On this site, Bob DeMarco details his 24-7 care of his mother, Dotty, addressing every aspect of eldercare. He supplements his own views with articles on various subjects by other experts, and thousands of caregivers write to him to discuss candidly their experiences.

Gail Sheehy's book *Passages in Caregiving*[4] is thorough, thoughtful and especially useful when you reach the stage where, in your own mind, you begin to think of yourself not just as the One but the Only One.

Circumstances vary. Not everyone can afford to give up a job to become a full-time nurse and companion. Some do not have the physical or emotional strength to lift and bathe a partner. Some children live nearby; others are thousands of miles away, managing from a distance as best they can. Some bring to caregiving a history rich with love and lives well lived; others might have been in an abusive, sour relationship. Some see their role as a calling; others, like me, see it as a stage in their life, part of the cycle of loving. We bring who we have been all our lives to this new role, along with our previous relationship to the patient.

---

4   Gail Sheehy, *Passages in Caregiving, Turning Chaos into Confidence,* (New York: William Morrow, 2010).

Few, if any, of us are born saints. I would hope that we would be generous and nonjudgmental with each other and resist the temptation to think that there is only one good kind of caregiver. Except in cases of elder abuse, there is no right or wrong way to proceed. We do what we are emotionally, physically and financially capable of. Along the way, we discover the meaning of duty. And just when we think caregiver is a thankless role, there will be a radiant smile, the clasp of a hand, a gentle hug—the beauty in the duty.

A Love Story

THE ALZHEIMER'S WORLD IS A PARALLEL UNIVERSE—THE patient and the caregiver, the one who forgets and the one who is forgotten, the one whose memories recede and the one for whom those memories are the source of strength.

Ours was a second marriage for both. Given that I was 50 when we exchanged vows, the chances of celebrating our fiftieth wedding anniversary were few. So we decided we would live 50 years in the ones we had. At the outset, we both had work that sometimes meant travel. On those occasions, we were apart, but otherwise, we lived a life of togetherness.

We embraced each other's interests. I took up fly-fishing and developed sea legs for long weeks on a ketch on the coast of Maine. He found himself hosting a different group around the dinner table and going to cabaret and theatre openings. This was a marriage of true intimacy.

As a result, spending all my time with my husband after the diagnosis of dementia/Alzheimer's was an easy segue. But we would now spend time together differently. A reality check of things he could no longer do made it clear that I would have to take on extra family responsibilities and that we needed to develop a different pattern for our daily lives.

For a while, life did not change very much. Close friends came to dinner. He would have an occasional lunch with one of the young men he had mentored. I would deliver him to the meeting place, go on to lunch with a friend and then return to pick him up. His participation in conversation was limited, but he clearly enjoyed being with these special young people.

He was still physically strong and could walk a couple of city blocks using a cane, and we would go out to lunch together once or twice a week. We went to restaurants where the staff knew us and where we could sit beside each other. We would enjoy the restaurant scene, admire the girls, note the fashions and hold hands, and once, he put his arms around me and danced me out the door, to the applause of all the waiters.

For the first two years after hearing that dreadful word, *Alzheimer's*, I was the 7-day, 24-hour watchful wife and caregiver. During this time, we moved from a fairly normal routine to what I think of as the "prompt" months. He would wake up in the morning and before he even got out of bed would ask, "What should I be doing? Should I be doing something?" Prompted, he would get up for breakfast; prompted, he could shower and shave himself; and prompted, he could dress.

Then came another stage where even prompted, he could not do those things himself. The wife became the valet. I would tease him that I now had my own Ken doll, and he would laugh with me.

Others could see the changes in him more clearly than I could. And I began to hear a chorus of voices—family and friends— warning me that things would get worse, that I would not be able to manage on my own, that I should be thinking ahead, making a decision between home care or a nursing home. They told me that I needed to get away, take a break and have respite from the caregiving role. Eventually, I would face those decisions—I would decide on home care and not a nursing home, and I would recognize the need to take care of myself both physically and emotionally.

But at that time, I was not ready. My answer became more and more curt: "I am where I want to be, and I am doing what I want to do."

Am I a saint? No way. I never was a saint, and I never will be. The truth is, I was being selfish. During this period, there were times when my husband was very much himself. There would be humour, insight or affection. These moments were random and unpredictable, and I did not want to miss one of them, nor did I want to give up the physical intimacy of our morning bathing and shaving routine. My motivation for staying with him was as simple as that: total selfishness.

As these moments of clarity and mobility became less frequent, a terrible loneliness of the heart infected me. It was not a loneliness I could erase with an afternoon at the theatre with a friend. I was lonely for him—for our conversations, his strength and support, and all that we had shared. I was lonely for our marriage. His growing detachment was a hole in my life that no one else—nothing else—could fill.

In this universe of parallels, while his memory was fading, it was my rich memory bank that sustained me and gave me strength. Those memories were also the source of my pain—constant reminders of how much this thief called Alzheimer's had stolen from me.

Know Thy Enemy

DIANA, PRINCESS OF WALES, ONCE SAID THAT THERE WAS A third person in her marriage. There was a third entity in my marriage too—not another woman, but Alzheimer's disease (AD).

Once I recovered from the shock of the diagnosis, I decided to learn as much as I could about this disease that was stealing my husband's identity and robbing me of a beloved partner bit by bit. Let me share with you what I, as a caregiver and a member of the board of overseers of the Alzheimer's Drug Discovery Foundation (ADDF), have learned. You might want to check some sources for yourself, and I recommend the websites of the Alzheimer's Association, the Alzheimer's Society Toronto, the National Institute on Aging, as well as that of the Alzheimer's Drug Discovery Foundation.

First, what is Alzheimer's? Dementia is a weakening of memory and cognitive function. There are several types of dementia, but Alzheimer's is the most common, and it is a progressive, fatal, neurodegenerative disease. If you think we have only recently started to hear much about AD, you are correct. It acquired a name in 1906, when a German physician, Dr. Alois Alzheimer, performed an autopsy on a patient who had died after several years of memory loss and confusion. The autopsy revealed the plaques and tangles that are now considered the definitive factors leading to a diagnosis of AD.

However, although Alzheimer's had acquired a name, it was not until the 1970s that the medical profession formally recognized it as a disease and not as just a normal part of aging. Even then, doctors diagnosed the condition only when the patient was in the last, visible stage of dementia, and then an autopsy confirmed the diagnosis. Over the past quarter of a century, the medical and scientific worlds gradually determined that there are three progressive stages through Alzheimer's:

a)   the preclinical
b)   mild cognitive impairment
c)   dementia

The increase in numbers of AD patients is partly because diagnoses now take place earlier in the progression and also because, as a generation, we are living longer.

We now know that Alzheimer's takes root in the brain a decade or more before any symptoms are present. There are two types: early-onset and late-onset. About 5 percent of AD patients have early-onset Alzheimer's, an uncommon form of dementia that strikes people before age 65, in some cases in their forties and fifties. Although the symptoms as the disease progresses are the same, early-onset AD often runs in families and is likely to be linked to a mutation in one of three genes: the APP, PSEN 1 or PSEN 2.

Late-onset AD is associated with a different gene. Dr. Howard Fillit cites the presence of ApoE as the "most significant genetic risk factor for late-onset AD. A certain type of ApoE (ApoE E4) increases the risk before age 75 up to 20 fold." Although testing for this gene is not part of a routine blood analysis, genetic testing can be requested and could provide valuable information to those with a family history of AD. Dr. Fillit points out, "The odds of getting AD increase four-fold if one of your parents has it; probably at least double that if both parents do."

What causes it? Apart from family history and genetics, most scientists agree that there are many other factors that might contribute to or trigger AD. The list includes age, presence of type 2 adult diabetes, mild cognitive impairment, environment, head injury and lifestyle. Alzheimer's is not an inevitable result of aging, but the chances of occurrence do increase with age. The statistics are scary: One person in eight over the age of 65 and one in three over the age of 80 will get Alzheimer's disease.

The brain is part of the body, so protecting it means observing the rules set out for general good health. Just as an unhealthy lifestyle might make you vulnerable to other diseases, it might also make you a candidate for Alzheimer's. But the right choices in diet, exercise and intellectual stimulation do not necessarily inoculate you.

Ronald Reagan had a supportive family, interesting work, and the best medical care available and was physically fit, but he died of Alzheimer's. My husband also lived a healthy and happy life that included tennis, fly-fishing, sailing, engaging work and family and friends who cared for him. At 70, he could still wear the white tie and tails he wore when he was a Princeton undergraduate. Still, he would die from complications of Alzheimer's.

How is Alzheimer's diagnosed? In most instances, the family physician, consulted by the patient or a concerned family member, will make the diagnosis. The primary-care doctor might then recommend a visit to a geriatric specialist or a neurologist. Diagnostic testing will probably include such challenges as memorizing a list of names, word association, drawing a clock and counting backward.

The doctor might suggest an MRI or a CT. While these tests do not definitively diagnose Alzheimer's, they, along with blood tests, can identify or rule out other possible causes for cognitive loss.

However, except for the genetic test mentioned above, which is mainly used in clinical trials to identify people with a higher risk, there is, at the moment, no blood test that will definitively identify Alzheimer's. In the United States, clinical trials of such a blood test are under way, based on research by Professor Michal Schwartz of the Weizmann Institute of Science. Initial trials in Israel showed the test to be 87 percent accurate, with an 85 percent specificity rate in detecting Alzheimer's and ALS (Lou Gehrig's disease).

ADDF provided critical seed funding for one of the most exciting new developments in diagnostic tools approved by the FDA for use in the United States. A radioactive dye called Amyvid, developed by Avid Pharmaceuticals and now part of the Eli Lilly and Company portfolio, makes possible for the first time a PET scan that will estimate beta-amyloid neuritic plaque density in adults experiencing some cognitive loss.

A negative scan would suggest that those problems are not the result of Alzheimer's but of some other factor. While a positive scan does not necessarily mean that the patient has AD, combined with other diagnostic tools, it can help doctors arrive at a more accurate assessment. That advance is only a start, but it is much more than we have had.

Is the disease fatal? Yes. Like many people, before I became part of the Alzheimer's world, I did not know that Alzheimer's kills. It does. Death by Alzheimer's results when the body forgets how to function. Millions are diagnosed with AD, and their average life span after diagnosis is seven years. None will survive.

Advice Unlimited

ONCE THE UNHERALDED AND FORGOTTEN GROUP, CAREGIVERS are now the subject of a cottage industry of advice. It pours at us in blogs, articles and books. Some say that you must enter the Alzheimer's world completely, forget all other aspects of self and become totally the caregiver, and others tell you that since the patient is "out of it," you might as well get on with your life.

I was too selfish to do the former and too much in love to believe the latter, so I bumbled along, taking each day as it came.

The most amusing advice that I received—over and over from assorted voices—was that I should see a therapist. *What*, I wondered, *did these people see when they looked at me?* Did I look terribly stressed? Was this suggestion a way of distancing themselves? Were they afraid I might unload my concerns on them? Or were they like so many in our society who think that every hardball life throws is something that should be taken to a therapist—that life should be happy, that there should be no downside? By all means, let's exorcise sadness from the lifecycle.

"It must be depressing," these people would say. Well, I was certainly sometimes sad, but I was not depressed. I draw a distinction between the two. Depression is a serious, debilitating, life-destroying illness that needs to be recognized, understood and treated. But sadness is simply a part of life. During our lifetimes, we will all meet events, situations and diagnoses that will make us sad. What kind of person would I be if watching what was happening to my husband did not make me sad? And every day was not filled with sadness. There were still hugs and moments of laughter.

Finally, though, I did listen to the voices, and I went to a therapist twice. This is why I would never make it as a politician—talking about myself and probing my various nerve ends for 50 minutes straight bores me to death. I was brought up in the Scots-Irish way—just get on with what you need to do. My credo is a version of the alcoholic's prayer—if you can change it, do so, if you can't, then so be it. Or as Winston Churchill is supposed to have said, "KBO"—keep buggering on.

Well, if talking to a therapist didn't help, why not a support group? I found online support groups to be a tremendous help. I could turn to them anytime—in the middle of the night if necessary—and skim through the various postings to find the ones that described situations similar to mine. I suspect that taking care of a parent is different in many ways from taking care of a spouse, so I looked for the experiences of other partners. Those postings provided me with a great learning lifeline.

But I did not personally attend a support group until a few months before my husband died. By that time, the caregiving was so intense that I needed the physical presence of other caregivers, the special understanding and comfort of group support. Until that point, when I did have some time to myself, I wanted to get away from the Alzheimer's world, to be with a friend and talk about books, politics and the theatre and catch up on the doings of other friends (yes, you may call that gossip!)—anything but Alzheimer's.

So I offer no advice. Each caregiver must find his or her own way. But I will share some things that have worked for me. Kitty Carlisle Hart once told me that she began every day by looking in the mirror and saying to her reflection, "I forgive you." That is not a bad way for any of us to start our days. I did that and I added to that plea, "Please give me the patience I need."

For me, patience was the hardest part of this role. I had always moved quickly, made decisions fast (sometimes too fast) and been prone to skip the small talk and get to the point. Ironically, I was married to a man who moved, thought and acted even more quickly than I did. Once, when he suggested we go for a walk, my answer would always be "Yes, if I don't have to run." Now his brain processed everything slowly, if at all, and he had become so physically frail that moving from A to B was a major effort.

So I started my day by forgiving myself for yesterday's impatience and praying for patience throughout the new one. May both be yours.

One Caregiver's Philosophy

In this Alzheimer's parallel universe, there are two concerns: the care of the patient and the care of the caregiver. Sometimes what is good for one is difficult for the other, but when a solution is found to a problem of the patient, life usually also gets better for the caregiver. As I said before, I don't presume to give advice. But let me share with you some approaches that have worked for me.

Like most caregivers, I began by playing catch-up. All I knew about Alzheimer's was the horrible stereotype of the patient. My husband was bewildered by the loss of some of his abilities. I was in shock. It took many months for me to absorb the diagnosis and come to terms with my new responsibilities and role.

I waited too long—two years—to get or accept help, only to find myself exhausted emotionally and physically. Then I had a kind of eureka moment: I realized that I was allowing myself as well as my husband to be at the mercy of Alzheimer's. I was just reacting; I needed to regain some control. My first source of help was the online support groups.

That exposure encouraged me to learn as much as I could about the disease, to try to understand what was happening to my husband. There are many excellent books, but my bible has been *The 36-Hour Day: A Family Guide to Caring for People with Alzheimer's Disease, Related Dementias, and Memory Loss.*[5] Knowledge and understanding made it possible for me to step back and view my role as a manager of my husband's well-being and care instead of a martyr forced to take care of him. It's a subtle distinction, but it helped me become a more-effective, less-stressed caregiver.

The medical profession divides Alzheimer's into three categories; the Alzheimer's Association breaks this down into seven stages. This kind of profiling is helpful in charting the progress of a patient as well as informing families and caregivers about what might lie ahead. But it is important to realize that Alzheimer's is not an assembly line: patients do not progress at the same speed through these stages. In my husband's case, he often straddled several Association stages at the same time, and there was considerable yo-yoing. One March, his condition deteriorated to the point where I was advised to arrange hospice; three weeks later, he rallied, and hospice was no longer appropriate.

If I could communicate only one thing through these blogs, it would be my belief that the Alzheimer's patient remains an individual. I firmly believe that the person you knew before AD is still in there. There are those who speak of personality changes. I wonder if that is a correct description. Is the person really changing, or is he or she understandably reacting to and against the toll of the disease?

---

5   Nancy L. Mace and Peter V. Rabins, *The 36-Hour Day: A Family Guide to Caring for People Who Have Alzheimer's Disease, Related Dementias, and Memory Loss* (Baltimore: Johns Hopkins Press Health Book).

Alzheimer's patients often *wander*. I put that word in italics because that is how it is described in various articles and books, giving the impression that it is movement without purpose. If you are the caregiver who must try to find a patient who has disappeared, the experience can be unnerving and frightening. Where could he or she have gone? Many communities now have developed ways to alert residents that a senior citizen has eluded a caregiver. But is that person really "wandering"? Could it be that deep inside, the patient needs to go somewhere? He or she might not know how to get there, but I suspect there is some purpose in the urge to move. Perhaps he wants to go home, or perhaps she just would like to get away from the hovering of others for a while. Our inability to understand what is going on in the mind of the Alzheimer's patient doesn't mean that there isn't something going on.

Others talk about anger as though it is an aberration. It seems to me that Alzheimer's patients have a lot to be angry about. Bit by bit, their control over themselves and their world is disappearing. The man who ran a major corporation can no longer button his own shirt. The woman whose greatest joy was to cook for her family can no longer follow a recipe.

When someone is in physical pain, we are not surprised if he or she howls. When my husband said to me, "Am I doing something wrong? Should I be doing something? Am I off my rocker?" he was expressing his anguish. When he railed at those trying to help him, he was fighting his dependence on others. If you stop to think about the level of frustration, confusion and agitation that AD patients are experiencing, their lashing out is understandable. Their anger is not personal; they are telling us of their pain. They are fighting not their caregivers but the disease. How should we react? It is tempting to take their behaviour personally, feel hurt or even get angry ourselves. But those responses accomplish nothing.

The caregiver won't feel better for expressing irritation—guilt is the inevitable by-product of loss of control.

We know that in the end, the battle with Alzheimer's is one that Alzheimer's will win. But the disease doesn't have to win every round. I tried to think of my husband and myself as partners in the fight. If I could turn away his anger with a hug, a smile or a word of understanding, we had won at least one round.

What works for one in terms of care might not work for all. But each of us—AD patient or not—is susceptible to tone of voice and facial expression. I could say to you, "Let's go," and whether you take it as an exciting invitation, a command or a scolding will depend on how I say it. The tone of voice means more than the actual words. Not the bark of a sergeant major and not baby talk, because the patient is not an infant—none of that "Have we had our bowel movement today?" Please!

When someone combines tone of voice with a smile or a scowl, one's reaction will likely mirror the presentation. So before I approached my husband about something that I wanted him to do—be it take a shower, come to the table for lunch or get ready to go to the doctor—I deliberately went into manager mode. I took a deep breath, got the tension out of my shoulders, thought about my tone of voice, lightened up my face and told myself to slow down, to accept his rhythm, his pace.

Tempering Temper

MY MOTHER USED TO START HER DAY BY SITTING ALONE IN the kitchen with a cigarette and a cup of tea. She called it "getting a handle on her day."

Well, I don't recommend the cigarette, but a caregiver definitely needs to "get a handle" on his or her day. As the day begins, so it usually unwinds, and tension begets tension.

I get a handle on my day by meditating. I started transcendental meditation (TM) about 35 years ago on the advice of a friend, and I have continued that ever since, except for during the first two years of my husband's Alzheimer's diagnosis. Foolishly, I told myself that with so many new challenges, I didn't have time for *that*. The truth was, I needed *that* more than ever.

There are many approaches to meditation, ranging from meeting with an instructor, going through the ritual of initiation and receiving a mantra, to learning about it from a book. Basically, meditation involves deep breathing, following the breath in and out. Thoughts may come and go, but you don't pay attention to them; you concentrate on your mantra or, depending on what method you are using, following the breath.

Our bodies are intricate, complicated machines made up of equally intricate, complicated parts interdependent on each other to function. But all parts are dependent on the simplest thing: breath. Breath is life. In a way, with each breath, we are recreating ourselves. TM helps me find my centre; it is known to lower one's blood pressure, and it provided me with deep rest when my night's sleep was almost always interrupted.

So half an hour before the dog, the husband and the house stirred, I got a handle on my day. That ritual preceded the ritual of caregiving. And ritual it must be. I found that a familiar routine was absolutely essential to a calm day—meals, bathroom, exercise, naps, bed at the same time every day. Change agitated my husband, so we tried to keep it to a minimum, and we gave him plenty of warning if something or someone new was on the schedule. However, I didn't tell him things too far ahead. That too caused agitation, as he would remember that I'd told him something but not what and would fret about what he had forgotten.

I typed up the day's schedule and gave it to him at breakfast. As he was once a foreign service officer, I hoped this routine might appeal to some deeply hidden sense of being given briefing papers. I noticed that he kept that piece of paper in his pocket and referred to it throughout the day, so I assume it gave him some sense of control. Although it did not completely do away with the repeated questions about the same things that can drive a caregiver mad, it cut down the number, and that made the day easier for me. And if I went out, he could refer to the note that told him where I was, whom I was with and when I would be back. This reassured him and saved his pride because he didn't have to ask for that information from others. As his progress through the disease accelerated, this was not as useful a tool as it once was, but it still helped.

If I were to provide caregivers with a collective mantra, it would be "Anticipate!" Look for the patterns. My husband had a hearing problem, and long before he was diagnosed with Alzheimer's, he would become irritated with people who did not speak clearly. Like many older people, he did not hear the high notes, so it was important to speak to him in a low-pitched voice—not loud, but low. Given the combination of poor hearing and the dementia, short declarative sentences were the best.

He would also lash out when people hovered over him, especially behind him, or when someone interfered with his independence. This was difficult, as we were concerned that he would fall. So we had to hover without seeming to hover and had to give him the chance to get up before we rushed to assist. But we could not wait so long to help that he tried something without success several times, as then he became angry with himself. It was an endless search for the tactful way.

Tact combined with respect for his dignity usually got results. If you took hold of his arm suddenly, he would resist and growl, "What are you doing?" But if you explained first what you were going to do, he would be compliant. I noticed that the great nurses not only told him what they were going to do but also asked for permission—for example, "May I take your blood pressure?"

Alzheimer's determined the pace of our days. You cannot hurry an Alzheimer's patient. I learned to take a laissez-faire approach to each day. If he didn't want to take a shower right away, fine, we'd do it later. I even learned to eat more slowly, because I noticed that when my plate was empty, my husband also stopped eating. As he had lost a lot of weight and needed to eat, I slowed down. That was good for him and for me. Years ago, I went to a spa in France where there was a sign on every table that said, "No matter how quickly you eat, the next course will not be served for 20 minutes."

I thought, *Look at it this way: I am not paying spa prices as I learn not just to eat but also to appreciate my food.*

So in short: To have a calm house, be calm. Keep to a regular routine. Anticipate the causes of agitation. Respect the patient's pace, abilities and dignity. Treat the patient the way all of us would like to be treated.

Caregiver Care

Do as I say and not as I did. That's the subtext of these suggestions to other caregivers.

Yes, when I write about how a caregiver should take care of him- or herself, I am talking to myself as well as to others. When it comes to looking after yourself as well as the patient and scheduling the needed breaks away from caregiving, I plead mea culpa. Like many others, I postponed my own doctors' appointments, telling myself I didn't have the time, and turning down invitations from friends, believing that I was not only the One but the Only One.

So yes, I know how hard it is. For two years, I did not leave my husband. That was partly because I did not want to miss any of the moments of clarity that were left to us, partly because I felt responsible and partly because I was fearful that something would happen to him when I wasn't present. Kind but firm words from two doctor friends helped me decide to take the occasional afternoon for myself.

I am unlikely to ever forget the first time I took a break from his care. It was early in his staging. I wasn't comfortable about leaving him alone in the house, but he was offended that I had arranged for someone to stay with him. When I told him that the other person's presence was for me, that I would not be able to go unless I knew someone was on hand in case he fell, he acquiesced. That he was humouring his overprotective wife made the situation acceptable to his pride.

I am not likely to forget the betrayed look in his eyes—and those of our dog!—when I finally left. I swear that when I returned, they were both standing in the same places by the door, waiting for me with the same baleful looks on their faces. Over the years, my husband became more forgiving of my leaving from time to time. The dog, however, continues to give me that "How could you do this to me?" guilt trip whenever I leave him behind.

My husband did not like the first "sitter," because she insisted on chatting him up and trying to get him to play board games. Next time around, I did a better job of informing the stand-in caregiver about the established routine—lunch, a nap and then tea and a movie or television show, preferably *Foyle's War.* That series speaks to his generation, and he could watch it countless times. (I think I could repeat the scripts backward.)

I waited too long to take the occasional afternoon off and far too long—four years—to seek or accept regular help. As a result, I was exhausted, breaking the first and most important rule for the caregiver: stay healthy physically and emotionally. I urge you to seek the resources available—family, friends, the Visiting Nurse Association or their local equivalent. If you need help to find out what is available, get in touch with your local branch of the Alzheimer's Association. I was not "the Only One" who could take care of my patient: neither are you. Your break doesn't have to be a social occasion. A good walk can help you regain perspective. Swimming also does that for me. Exercise can be an excellent antidepressant.

Our dog, a little King Charles cavalier called Brewster, provided comfort and cheer to both of us. Yes, I know a dog is extra work, but oh my, it is worth it. On those days when my husband hardly said a word, he would still ask, "Where is Brewster?" Or if he couldn't remember the name, he'd say, "Where is our doggie?" Furthermore, my daily outings with this little guy, despite the stoop-and-scoop business, got me out of the house, mixing with other dog owners, and reminded me that there was a vibrant world available just outside the door.

And music—played at home or listened to in a church or synagogue or in a concert hall—offered real nourishment for my spirit. During the summer, I attended a Mostly Mozart concert with my daughter. As she lives 11 hours away, just being with her was magical. But being with her in an auditorium with hundreds of others, gathered together for the sole purpose of listening to beautiful music, I found myself thinking there was hope for the world after all.

I discovered anew the truth in Congreve's words—the knots in my neck and shoulders were like the knots in the oak that he describes in this quotation:

> Musick has charms to sooth a savage breast
> To soften rocks or bend a knotted oak.

However difficult it might seem, dear fellow caregiver, I do hope that you will take steps to soften the rocks in your path and bend the knots of frustration and sorrow. Listen to the music of life. It awaits.

The Saints Among Us

THERE MIGHT BE SAINTS AMONG US, BUT I AM NOT ONE OF them.

One does not usually associate the word *lucky* with Alzheimer's disease. But within the world of almost 8 million North American families struggling with the emotional and financial costs of this terrible disease, I have been lucky in many ways.

I was lucky that although my husband could get angry, he did not exhibit the rage that some caregivers experience. I was lucky because I didn't have to juggle caregiving with a job. I was lucky that, until the end, he still recognized me. I was lucky there were resources that permitted me to keep him at home with some part-time help—although it is frightening how fast one runs through those resources! Above all, I was lucky I came to this role from a great marriage rich with memories that were sources of strength.

What, I wonder, *would one do if the marriage hadn't been good?* What if your partner had been abusive or betrayed you? Where would you find the grace and generosity of spirit to take on the duty? Even with my strong feelings for my husband, I sometimes found myself wondering how long this arrangement could go on. If I didn't still care about him, if we hadn't shared a foundation of love and laughter, where would I have found the patience? If there are saints among the caregivers, the partners who rise to this occasion despite a stormy history are surely candidates.

I am also lucky that by the time Alzheimer's claimed my husband he was an elder statesman. While one has to regret that he spent his last years on earth struggling with this illness, there is some comfort in knowing that he lived a full life on his own terms, with nothing left on what Hollywood calls "the bucket list." And I too was at an age where, as lonely as it was, I was not sacrificing anything. I'd lived a good, happy and productive life.

I loved, and I was loved. This was[6] just another chapter. But if we had known—and oh, who knew what a big word *if* could be?—and had received advance notice of the disease, we might have taken one last trip, visiting old friends and old haunts, retracing our own footsteps, consciously celebrating the time we had shared together. But wishing for that is simply greed; what we had was more than enough.

So I think of the other families in which Alzheimer's has claimed someone still in the midst of life, perhaps before the person reached his or her potential, before there was time to create some financial stability, let alone forge a memory bank like ours. How do those partners come to terms with such a cruel fate? If there are saints among the caregivers, we can find them there. And what of those who have no private financial resources? How do they cope? It is beyond imagining.

And what of the children asked to take care of their parents? What of the child drafted in midlife into the role because he or she is an only child, the one who is geographically the closest, the only one who doesn't have a job or the one everyone always looks

---

6   http://www.hindawi.com/journals/ecam/2012/927509.

to? This responsibility calls for putting one's life on hold, often for years. This timing of AD causes additional pain in all directions— no parent would knowingly ask such a sacrifice of his or her child. While becoming a caregiver might be ennobling, it is still life, interrupted.

As if that isn't enough, what if there are unresolved issues between parent and child? What if we are asked to care for a parent we do not like or perceive as having judged us or treated us unfairly? A parent who has abused us emotionally or physically? Can we care for someone if we don't care about him or her? These are the real side effects of Alzheimer's—reaching out in endless circles to cut off lives beyond those of the patients.

I ask a lot of questions for which I have no answers. Perhaps some of you do.

What I do know is that we all share in the knowledge that Alzheimer's is a disease of the brain that is paid for with the currency of the heart.

Eight Steps to a
Healthy Brain

MY GRANDMOTHER'S REMEDY FOR EVERYTHING WAS CASTOR oil. The thought of it cured a lot of ailments. Faced with a choice of castor oil or going to school, we went to school.

In their book, *Cognitive Decline: Strategies for Prevention,*[7] Dr. Howard M. Fillit and Dr. R.N. Butler outline some ways to keep our brains healthy. Although there is no guarantee that following their suggestions will prevent Alzheimer's, they are not castor oil. Far from tasting bad, they will improve your life as you are living it. If they also turn out to prevent this disease, that's a big bonus. Dr. Fillit tells us that "cognitive impairment with aging is preventable" and that "through lifestyle interventions and effective management of chronic medical conditions, attaining and maintaining cognitive health is possible."

When Dr. Fillit talks or writes, I listen. He is one of my Alzheimer's heroes. In addition to his role with the Alzheimer's

---

[7]   Cognitive Decline: Strategies for Prevention. Fillit H.M. and Butler, R.N., (London, Greenwich Medical Media, 1997)

Drug Discovery Foundation, he has a distinguished academic career at Rockefeller University and the Mount Sinai School of Medicine in New York, where he is a clinical professor. The author or coauthor of more than 300 scientific and clinical publications, he is the senior editor of *Textbook of Geriatric Medicine and Gerontology*. To all that scientific background, he brings the personal knowledge gained in his private practice. He is one of the few doctors who combine scientific knowledge with real experience with patients, and he also has firsthand knowledge of the caregiver's burden: his own father recently died from AD.

Dr. Fillit points out that some medical illnesses—among them hypertension, high cholesterol, obesity, thyroid issues, diabetes and, in men, low testosterone—are associated with diminished cognitive function, so the first of his recommended eight actions is to control those health issues. The second is to follow a balanced, low-fat, low-calorie diet. He recommends a multivitamin every day as well as the clinically tested DHA, a component of omega-3, which is available online. He adds, "Vitamin D deficiency, very common in older people, is not only bad for the bones, but also the brain. Older people should get their Vitamin D levels checked and, if low, should take supplements." A B12 deficiency is also common among older people, and if low, Dr. Fillit recommends supplements that are usually in the form of once-a-month injections. He suggests you keep alcohol intake to a maximum of two drinks a day, and if you have already been diagnosed with mild cognitive decline (MCI), he recommends you cut out alcohol completely.

Sleep is a component of his eight-point strategy. He offers some tips on getting a good night's sleep, one of which, surprisingly, is to avoid sleeping pills. Instead, he recommends having a glass of warm milk and avoiding eating and exercising three hours before bedtime. Pointing out that depression might cause memory loss and difficulty paying attention, Dr. Fillit urges family members or friends to encourage those who are depressed, anxious, grieving or lonely to seek help. He suggests that seniors plan for a postretirement life that keeps them involved socially and connected to their communities as well as their families.

Dr. Fillit recommends exercise—for the body and the brain. He suggests moderate-intensity aerobic exercise for at least 30 minutes three to five days per week. As for the brain, he recommends continued use through adult education, particularly learning something new. He says, "Learning to play a musical instrument, reading books or a new language will all promote cognitive health." He lists mind games as another possible way to promote cognitive health but adds that "They have not been proven to have generalized benefits on daily function."

Dr. Fillit also discusses the effects of stress on the body, including muscle tension, elevated heart rate, higher blood pressure and the secretion of stress hormones. The result can be fatigue, disturbed sleep, poor concentration and memory lapses. He concludes, "Chronically high levels of stress hormones suppress the immune system and kill brain cells. Older adults with a high level of psychological distress have twice the risk of cognitive impairment."

He lists eight ways to cope with stress, one of which is meditation. One recent study approved by the University of Virginia Review Board links meditation and AD. Results of the study—by K. E. Innes, T. K. Self, C. J. Browne, K. M. Rose and A. Thompson Heisterman—were published in *Evidence-Based Complementary and Alternative Medicine*, volume 2012.[8] It was among the first to investigate the effects of meditation on caregivers or AD

---

8   The Effects of Meditation on Perceived Stress and Related Indices of Psychological States and Sympathetic Activation in Persons with Alzheimer's Disease and Their Caregivers: A Pilot Study, Volume 2012.

patients and its authors explained: "Community dwelling adults with a diagnosis of mild cognitive impairment (MCI) or early-stage Alzheimer's Disease, together with their caregivers were enrolled." They were asked to meditate for 11 minutes twice daily for 8 weeks. The participants "demonstrated improvement in all major outcomes including perceived stress, mood, depression, sleep, retrospective memory function, and blood pressure."

This advice is definitely not castor oil and is definitely worth a try.

Saving the Elderly

I HAVE COME TO THE CONCLUSION THAT NO ONE REALLY understands old age until he or she gets there.

Indeed, society is busy denying that old age exists. We are told that 70 is the new 50—to which I say, "Nonsense." Perhaps 70 is the new 70; people might look younger and have more vitality (especially if they are affluent) than a 70-year-old did years ago. But the body, however well it has been cared for, is still 70. Brain cells have been dying, bones have changed, discs have grown closer together and the skin is thinner. Like it or not, old age awaits.

The lack of understanding of the reality of old age is apparent when a big storm hits a community. Orders go out to evacuate, and those who give the orders are shocked when older people don't obey and instead decide to stay in their homes and ride out the storm. They are scolded publicly, accused of putting others at risk.

Why don't these stubborn old folks readily obey and leave their homes?

My husband and I lived through several major storms, two of them after he was diagnosed with Alzheimer's. Both times, we were advised to move, and like many other seniors, we decided to stay put. When I made that decision, I knew that we were in danger, and I did not expect anyone—fireman, policeman or National Guard—to rescue us from that danger. I made the decision fully aware of the consequences. Had one of our grandchildren been staying with us that would have been different. I would have found a way to get him or her to safety. But just us, two old folks comfortable with whatever life might bring?

Why would we leave our home? Where would we go? How do you take a spouse who has Alzheimer's, whose stability depends on an unchanging routine, to a shelter filled with strangers, noise and confusion and ask him or her to spend who knows how many hours, perhaps days, in an alien, frightening environment? How do you explain the need to do that to someone who can no longer comprehend the simplest things?

When those in authority order seniors to evacuate, they fail to understand what it is to be senior—to have to go the bathroom several times a night, to have an unsteady gait and poor balance, to have lost peripheral vision, to not be able to hear. Meet these older folks, and see what they are really like.

You might know a 90-year-old who is sharp as the proverbial tack, still drives and lives an independent life. However, for everyone like that, there are the others whose arthritic bones move slowly and who think slowly, process information slowly and make decisions slowly. They move with an array of stuff. Every aging body carries with it all or a combination of the following: dentures; distance and reading glasses; hearing aids and batteries; medications, some of which have to be taken several times a day; ointment for thin, easily bruised skin; diapers; a cane, walker or wheelchair; oxygen; catheters and injections. The thought of trying to move all that with help, let alone by yourself or with an ailing partner—to say nothing of bringing along a dog, cat or bird—is surely daunting.

Let me tell you, old age is definitely not for sissies.

We can't begin to care for the aged in emergencies unless we understand and accept what aging really means. If all the baby boomers who are approaching their senior years actually believe that 70 is the new 50, they are in for a big surprise. And unless we drastically change our approach to protecting seniors in emergencies, they too will likely find they are also defying authority, staying in their own homes, surrounded by all their paraphernalia, and saying, "Damn the consequences."

Old Folks Talking

I DON'T HAVE ANY DESIRE TO BE YOUNG AGAIN. LIKE THE majority of older people, I believe the world I experienced was the best one. I have no desire to tweet, have a phone hanging like an umbilical cord from my ear or walk around town wearing what looks like long underwear.

But I do envy one aspect of being young: youth is the only time in your life when you are confident that you know everything. I remember when I was young, when I knew everything. Way back then, when I saw an old couple in a restaurant, sitting throughout a meal without apparently offering a word to each other, I used to think, *How awful*, and I would vow to myself that I would never be a partner in a marriage like that—two people with nothing to say to each other. *How terrible*. How little I knew.

From time to time, many of those who knew about my husband's Alzheimer's asked me, "Do you have any conversation at all with him?" Well, that depends on how you define *conversation*. We did not have conversations like the ones we used to have, which began at breakfast with the arrival of three newspapers and started with a discussion of Washington, Ottawa, New York and Toronto politics.

My husband set an intellectual pace with his knowledge of politics and economics, and the breakfast talk would be one in which I felt challenged to think and rethink. Then, typically, we would part ways and not see each other again until late in the day, when we would tell each other about our days, discuss what we had heard and learned and touch on family and finances. If we were going out to dinner, we would discuss where and with whom and, if I had initiated the guest list, why, and if we were staying home, we would talk about what we were going to eat. The latter discussion could take quite a long time. And so it would go from breakfast until the lights went out, and the last words would be "Good night. I love you."

I miss all that beyond mere words, and I have found that words are just that—mere.

During the last three years of my husband's illness, days could go by when my husband did not say a word, let alone comment on the world outside our doors. But that did not mean that we didn't have conversations. We did. There is a kind of silent communication that is as powerful as any based on speech. He could tell me with his eyes that he appreciated what I did for him. He could tell me with a smile that he was pleased to be with me. Without a word, he could let me know that he was unhappy because I was going out, leaving him behind.

When it was a really good day, if I asked him if he loved me, he would say yes, and when I asked why, sometimes—rarely but sometimes—he would still answer, as he used to do, "Damned if I know." And always, if I told him, "I love you," he would answer, "Thank you. I love you too."

Does anyone really need any more than that?

I have learned to look at that old couple in the restaurant and see them in a different way. Perhaps they don't have anything to say to each other anymore. When you have lived a long time, the world around you tends to repeat itself. You have said everything you could say—more than once. There truly isn't much new under the sun. So the general had an affair. Remember, so did Ike! Or so it was said.

But it is also possible that such a couple has moved beyond words, that what pulses between them is so strong, so deeply rooted, so much a matter of fact that it just is. When you look at them, you might indeed be seeing what it looks like to be an old married couple. And you might realize that is not something to pity but is a state perhaps even to envy later, when, with age, you find that you don't know much, let alone everything.

The Rivers of My Memory

GLEN CAMPBELL COAXED OUR FEET TO MOVE, OUR HIPS TO sway, and he touched our hearts and made us smile with "A Rhinestone Cowboy" and "By the Time I Get to Phoenix" and, perhaps prophetically, with the lyrics "By the rivers of my memory, ever smiling, ever gentle, on my mind."

Prophetic because the rivers of Campbell's memory are receding. Glen Campbell has joined the list of millions diagnosed with Alzheimer's disease. He has been saying good-bye to his many fans on a farewell tour and recently issued a new album—its title, *Ghost on the Canvas*, will resonate with anyone who understands the nature of Alzheimer's disease. Oscar-winning producer James Keach has created a documentary about Campbell's battle with Alzheimer's, which is being shown at Alzheimer's fundraisers all over America.

Campbell's family have joined the circle of loving partners, children, and friends who must watch helplessly as AD steals bits and pieces of the brain and identity of a man beloved not just by them but also by country-music lovers all over the world. They are helpless because there is no effective treatment and no cure—not for Glen Campbell or anyone else who is in the darkening web of

Alzheimer's. All we who love them and treat them can do—and it is a lot—is provide loving care and comfort and try to change the future for the next generation.

In a letter, Campbell's daughter Ashley, one of three of his children accompanying him on his farewell tour, wrote,

> I was in high school when my father, Glen Campbell, started having trouble remembering things. Soon after, in early 2011, the doctor told our family that he had Alzheimer's disease.
>
> While performing on tour with my dad this past year, I have seen firsthand how this terrible disease slowly creeps in. It is stealing a devoted father from his family and a beloved talent from the world.
>
> My dad keeps saying to me, "I love you, I love you so much." I realize that soon he might not know that he loves me because he won't know who I am. So I do everything I can right now to let him know I love him since there's not much more I can do. There are no drugs available today to prevent, treat, or cure Alzheimer's.
>
> But there is hope. My family and I are partnering with Leonard Lauder and the Alzheimer's Drug Discovery Foundation (ADDF) to help fast track drug research—if not in time for my father, then for the many others that will follow.

I have not met Ashley Campbell, but I share her heartache and her determination to bring hope to the next generation. And like her, I have embraced the work of ADDF. Founded by Leonard and Ronald Lauder, ADDF's only mission is to accelerate the discovery of drugs to prevent, treat and cure AD, related dementias and cognitive aging. In explaining his passion for the cause, Leonard Lauder once told me that (unlike a lot of other rich people) he has no interest in having a building or a wing with his name engraved on it. What he wants is a cure and better treatment for AD in his lifetime.

ADDF is structured as a venture philanthropy model—grants are given as investments so that if a project comes to market, ADDF shares in the profits, which are then reinvested in new research grants. You can learn more about ADDF on its website, alzdiscovery.org. For now, you might want to thank Glen Campbell for all the moments he shared with you through his music by making a donation in his name. ADDF is a registered charity in both the United States and Canada, and contributions may be sent to the Alzheimer's Drug Discovery Foundation, 57 West 57th Street, New York, NY 10019, marked "Glen Campbell tribute."

How Are You, Mom?

J UST IN FRONT OF EVERY BABY BOOMER, THERE IS A PARENT— or parents. Like me, these parents are on the brink of old age and all that aging brings.

Let us suppose that I am your mother. Chances are, when you ask me, "How are you, Mom?" I will answer, "Fine."

Am I? Or am I in denial, protecting you from the truth, afraid to admit to my physical and mental lapses? Am I covering up? In the early stages of dementia or Alzheimer's, many are in denial to themselves and others, and they can be very good at faking and covering up lapses.

What do you know about me? I am not asking what you assume but what do you really know.

Let's do the factual check first. Have I identified someone as an emergency contact? Have I informed that person—and the rest of the family—about this decision? Is this information, along with my basic medical history, in my wallet? If that person is you, do you know the name and telephone number of my doctor? Are you up to date on my various diseases, illnesses and meds? Do I have a living will? Have I named a health-care proxy? Does the doctor have copies of this information? Do you? If you are the health-care proxy, are you prepared to say no to an insistent doctor if he or she wants to perform a procedure I want declined? Can you stand up to that pressure? Do you know your rights as a proxy? Are your siblings on board with my decisions and your obligation to enforce them? Have you had a family discussion about my aging process and what it might mean to everyone, not just me? Do you understand, respect, and accept, my end-of-life decisions?

Depending on where I live, do you know how much my old-age care might cost? What insurance do I have? If I want to remain independent in my own home, are there financial resources to support that? For how long? Who would be the caregiver? Have you discussed this with your siblings and/or stepsiblings? If I must go into assisted living or a nursing home, what do you know about the available facilities? Do you know what the government program would cover and what expenses would have to come from my income or from you and your siblings? Just when you finish paying for college, will you have to start paying for my old age?

Are you aware of the tests that are labeled ADLs (activities of daily living), the abilities people need to have in order to live by themselves? How do I rank? Can I bathe, dress, use the toilet myself, move without help and eat without assistance? Loss of two or three of those abilities is usually considered the qualification for admittance to a nursing home.

Now let's consider what I think of as the eyeball, or intuitive, check.

If you live far away, how often do you contact me? Do you know me well enough to recognize changes in my voice that might indicate a problem? Do you hear different things in my voice at different times of the day? If I don't answer the telephone for some time, whom would you call to check on me? When you were a teenager, your parents wanted to know who your friends were; in the same way, you need to know who your parents' friends are.

When you visit me, do you look at me? Closely? Am I as well groomed and carefully dressed as has been my habit? What pills are on my night table and in my medicine cabinet? Do you know that almost a third of all hospitalizations of elders are medication related? Have I lost weight? Do I seem frailer? What food is in the refrigerator? Are there new dents in the car? Do I seem to be overloaded with new magazine subscriptions? If so, I am probably the target of telemarketers; you might want to see what else I have been ordering. Is the chequebook in order? How much alcohol am I drinking? Do familiar objects seem to be missing?

Take a walk with me. How is my balance? My posture? Am I getting enough exercise? Do I still have a life outside my home? Do I have friends? Do I participate in activities? Have I been withdrawing from events and people I once embraced?

Are you prepared to step in to ask these questions and have this discussion before there is a crisis? I might welcome your taking over some of my responsibilities. Yes, I might be testy, even angry, at the suggestion that I can't manage everything myself. I am the parent, and you are the child. I might resist. But in my heart, I hope that you will continue to push, because I know in my brain that if we face the problems of my aging as a family, we will make better, more-informed, less-pressured decisions and that when I die, as I must, you will have no remorse and I will have the good death that each of us prays for.

A Diverting Affair?

THERE ARE NOT MANY BOOKS OR ARTICLES THAT DEAL frankly with the special psychological and emotional issues encountered by the caregiver whose patient is a spouse. Dr. Ruth Westheimer honestly and accurately discusses this issue for gay and straight partners in her new book, *Dr. Ruth's Guide for the Alzheimer's Caregiver.*[9]

She understands the nature of our loneliness. Although she is not and never has been a caregiver herself, she has drawn on her life experiences and the advice of many experts to produce a book that would be of interest to anyone starting out in the caregiver role. It's a thorough summary of the nature of the disease, its effects on family, and various medical and legal issues, and she makes some practical suggestions that are helpful.

However, when I read the parts related to her specialty—sex—I didn't know whether to laugh or cry, so I did both. First, she gives caregivers permission to have an affair: "If you need

---

9   Dr. Ruth K. Westheimer with Pierre A. Lehu, *Dr. Ruth's Guide for the Alzheimer's Caregiver* (Fresno, California: Quill Driver Books, 2012).

the companionship, the love, and yes, the sexual gratification of a relationship, then by all means, seek one out."

And although she is careful to say she is not advocating infidelity, there are instances when she certainly seems to be: "If your spouse is much older than you, or if your spouse has early-onset Alzheimer's, that's an even stronger reason to look for a new partner."

Now, if seeking outside comfort in another partner is indeed your desire, I don't think you need Dr. Ruth's permission—or anyone else's—and I will not judge you. It's entirely your business.

But I would like you to tell me how you find the time, energy and emotion.

I am not Brooke Astor, who once told me she put herself to sleep by counting the men she had slept with. But way back when, before I married this man, I did have an affair or two. I didn't count then, and I won't count now.

Perhaps affairs have changed in the intervening 30-odd years. But what I remember is that they took some planning—phone calls, notes, coded glances across dining room tables, the pressure of a knee, discussions of "Your place or...?" Certainly not mine. Not now.

Once those details are out of the way, there is the matter of pretty lingerie, body cream and pedicures. I have never known a woman having an affair who did not put great emphasis on having a pedicure. I'm not sure why. Do we walk into the bedroom on our hands, waving our feet? I think not. But an affair without a pedicure is unthinkable. And then there is perfume in private places. I was at a loss as to how any of that would have fit into my day.

Getting away is always difficult for an adulterer, but for the caregiver, it's a special problem. My cell phone was attached to my hip. Do you leave your cell phone on during your intermezzo? What if the aide left in charge needs to call you? Never mind the existential question of how you live with yourself if your partner dies while you are occupied this way. What about the practical matters? Do you come back smelling musky? Or with wet hair?

Perhaps if your partner is in a nursing home, the practical stuff is easier. But I don't know any caregiver who is actually giving care who would have the energy or the emotion required for an affair. I certainly didn't. The idea was laughable.

Dr. Ruth also makes finding this new partner sound easy: "No matter what your age, you'll benefit from having some companionship … the fact is, if you want the companionship from a relationship, you probably are going to have to accept the entire package which will include a sexual component."

Step right up to the partnership buffet, dear friends—will you have sex as a side? Dr. Ruth should meet some of the widows and divorcees I know: attractive women who are engaged in the community, meeting people. They're in better, less-complicated positions than caregivers and probably taking better care of themselves. They might even have regular pedicures. However, even when using online services, they tell me that finding that *"someone"* is difficult. Perhaps it's easier for the men. There are more women available. But for the most part, the men are looking for younger partners—future caregivers perhaps?

There is something about this casual approach that I find offensive all around. First, it shortchanges the affair. What you want from such a relationship, dear touch-hungry caregiver, is clear. What do you have to give? And once started, what makes you think you will be able to control where the relationship goes? At my age, a new companion would probably be on the brink of needing caregiving himself. About this, I am definitely with Stephen Sondheim: I am not doing it twice.

But above all, participating in an affair misunderstands the power of a true marriage. Now, I realize that Alzheimer's does not specialize in happy relationships. If you chose to be a caregiver when the relationship was not happy, then I am all the more admiring of your sense of duty. The idea of fidelity—and the dimension it brings to a relationship—might have been erased long before your partner's diagnosis with AD. Each of you might have already been going your separate way physically and emotionally.

But that is not always the case—it certainly was not in mine. Did I miss lovemaking after my husband and I were no longer physically intimate? Yes—emphatically, yes. Even though I had paid aides, I often gave my husband his shower, because I needed the physical intimacy of touch. We still slept together. Sometimes that meant I didn't get a good night's sleep. But the sense of him beside me, the sound of his breathing and the knowledge that I could sometimes quiet his distress with a stroke of my hand on his arm outweighed the sleepless nights. We were bound together by something greater than sex, greater than love—something so powerful it was beyond words. This connection was stronger now than it was seven years ago when we entered the parallel universe of Alzheimer's.

Although he was slipping away from me, I believe that if I'd had an affair, he would have known. He would have sensed it. I knew that perhaps, as it did for Justice Sandra Day O'Connor, the day might come when a nursing home was the right place for my husband. And perhaps, like hers, my husband would find another partner in the dementia world. As he would then have entered into the amoral oblivion of amnesia, there would be no question of anger or jealousy or outrage on my part. I would be glad that he had found some pleasure in that foggy universe.

According to Dr. Ruth, that would have be my Get out of Jail Free card. But I would not have entered into oblivion: I would still possess and be possessed by memory. And now that I have experienced this mingling of body, mind and spirit, I am not in the market for anything less.

Why Know?

Most of us prefer to delay bad news. But when it comes to Alzheimer's disease, the earlier the diagnosis, the better—for the patient and the prospective caregiver.

An early diagnosis of mild cognitive impairment, or first-stage Alzheimer's, gives the patient some control. He or she can make lifestyle changes—get more exercise, drink less alcohol, eliminate the use of sleeping pills, among other things—that might slow down the progress of the disease. Patients can find ways to say what needs to be said to family and friends while there is still time. Early-stage patients also have the option to enroll in pilot studies or clinical trials, which might benefit them and certainly will help develop better treatment.

If the patient doesn't already have a living will and a health-care proxy or power of attorney, this is the time to see a lawyer. And perhaps most importantly, the patient can take an active role in developing the plan the patient and family must have in order to meet the demands of the coming years.

For the caregiver, an early diagnosis means time to digest the news—to understand and accept the mountain of responsibilities that lie ahead. In every partnership, there is an informal distribution of duties. One pays the bills, and another does the shopping; one puts out the garbage, and the other looks after the car; one organizes family gatherings, and the other makes the travel arrangement; one cooks, and the other carves. However all that falls out, you will find yourself doing everything you have always done, plus everything your partner did, in addition to learning to be a caregiver.

If, like me, you lived in a cocoon about family finances, you need to learn everything there is to know: details of insurance (private and government), sources of income and the names of agents, accountants and bank officials, and passwords. There is a sharp learning curve to climb before you even begin the real duties of the caregiver. Let us hope that this diagnosis comes when your loved one is still capable of participating in a discussion about the future. There is no right or wrong way to proceed—just what is right for you and the patient.

This is the time to examine yourself and accept your capabilities and your weaknesses. It is also the time for important decisions. Are you going to want to stay in your home? If so, what would the eventual costs of that be? What resources are available? Can you do it? The time will come when you will need extra hands. Is family available, or will you need to hire aides? What resources are there in the community to help? Or is this the time to move to some type of assisted living or turn to a nursing home? What facilities are available, and what questions do you need to ask? Jane Gross's book *A Bittersweet Season, Caring for Our Aging Parents—And Ourselves*[10] is an excellent source of information on this subject.

---

10   Jane Gross, *A Bittersweet Season, Caring for Our Aging Parents—And Ourselves* (New York: Vintage, 2012).

You should learn everything you can about the disease, its stages and its treatments. Knowledge is more important than hope. Scam artists and fake cures follow in the wake of every ailment, AD among them. We would all like to think there is an easy cure. There isn't. That doesn't mean that there are no treatments available that will make the inevitable progress of the disease more comfortable for the patient and the caregiver—there are. As the gatekeeper to your patient's care, you need to be able to differentiate between scientific fact and false hope.

An early diagnosis also permits a thorough examination of the medical care available. Is your family physician willing to take on this illness to the end? Does he or she have the patience to care for someone whose cognitive abilities are declining? You can't fit an AD patient (or any elderly person) into a 20-minute appointment. This might be the moment when you have to seek out a geriatric specialist. Unfortunately, there are not many. As a result, it is not uncommon for a 90-year-old to be put on a waiting list at a geriatric service—surely that is one definition of *irony*!

No matter which doctor you choose to guide you through this disease, as caregiver, you are going to be the major coordinator. You can't count on the various services to remember the details of the patient's medications and medical issues. You must be on top of the information at all times, and you should carry this information in your wallet.

In terms of defining care, you and your partner should discuss frankly the types and levels of procedures the patient considers acceptable. Alzheimer's rarely requires the kind of radical intervention commonly dealt with in a living will. But you will be dealing with not only AD but also the process of aging and an accumulation of additional, treatable health issues. How much treatment should the patient receive? Should there be heart surgery?

How many tests for various diseases should medical professionals administer? As the AD patient's intellectual capacity declines, these decisions will become yours alone to make. It is a lonely road.

I highly recommend the book *My Mother, Your Mother, What to Expect as Parents Age*.[11] Although Dennis McCullough wrote this book for adult children taking on the care of a parent, in its advocacy of slow medicine, it is a useful guide for anyone caring for a patient with an incurable disease. This book is an impassioned call to "preserve the quality of life, even in the face of difficult and accumulating diseases." Reading it was a eureka moment for me. I realized that because I felt that I had to be doing something, I was taking my husband to too many doctors and pursuing too many unnecessary treatments. I relaxed, and life became a lot easier for both of us.

Sometimes I think that the only thing that matches the number of new medical treatments is the growing list of things we wouldn't want done to us in an emergency room. I appreciate the fact that doctors want to save lives. But in some cases, the patient should be allowed to go peacefully into that good night. That is a decision you and your partner—and only the two of you—can make while there is time.

---

11 Dennis McCullough, MD, *My Mother, Your Mother What to Expect as Parents Age* (Boston: Harper Collins, 2008).

As Time Goes By

As WE ENTERED THE SEVENTH YEAR OF LIVING WITH Alzheimer's, my husband was the patient, but the circle of those who suffered because of that diagnosis was large.

- The grandchildren, whom he might or might not remember. When he didn't, how could one soften that blow?
- The young men who once looked to him for advice and mentoring who now tried to bring the outside world to him, only to find a man whose focus was somewhere out there in the fog of the middle distance. Sometimes he recognized them; increasingly often, he faked it.
- Caregivers, sometimes abused by a man whose default mode was once that of a gentleman. He might have berated the president of a bank but never the clerk.
- His family members, lonely for evidence of a connection to a shared past.

And I—wife, lover, friend, companion, partner—like my husband, I lived in a half world. He was there, and he was not there.

I knew so little. And I wanted our reality to be not so. The past seven years had been years of learning, facing the inevitability of age and what aging means and stretching myself to accept new responsibilities. I was no longer the only caregiver, and every day, I blessed the two members of our team, Martha and Gene, for the compassion, humour and attentiveness they brought to their roles. They watched over both of us, pushed me out the door when I needed to get away and turned the growls to smiles.

Long before the Alzheimer's Association defined the seven stages of the disease, Shakespeare described the seven stages of man:

> All the world's a stage and all the men and women
> merely players;
> And one man in his time plays many parts,
> His act being seven stages.

Shakespeare's stages include that of the infant, the whining schoolboy, the lover, the soldier, the justice "full of wise saws" and the "lean and slippered pantaloon," and he concludes,

> Last scene of all that ends this strange eventful
> history
> Is second childhood and mere oblivion,
> Sans teeth, sans eyes, sans taste, sans everything.[12]

For me, until then, there had been two additional stages: before and after the heart attack. Before, the Alzheimer's progressed quite slowly; his concentration had not been what it was, and he'd needed to be prompted to do things and helped to execute some, but we had a life. Then, at the start of the sixth year, he had a heart attack on the

---

12 William Shakespeare, *As You Like It*, Act 2, Scene 7.

street and was taken by ambulance to the hospital, where he received excellent care. But he never recovered from that hospital stay.

His decline, both mental and physical, accelerated after that. I am told that this is a common experience—that a patient's post-treatment decline is not a comment on the procedure (whatever it might be) or its success. It's a variation on that old saying "the operation was a success, but the patient died"—the hospitalization did what it was supposed to do, but it left the patient weaker and more disoriented. It is not the fault of the doctors, nurses or surgeries; it is the hospital experience itself—lights, noises, strange faces, voices, disturbed sleep—and the consciousness such an environment brings that life is, for all of us, in the balance.

After that incident, we dealt with the yo-yo progress of AD, plus the inevitable decline that is part of aging. Exactly one year after that heart attack, we moved to a third—and, as it turned out, final—stage. Although he had not yet reached the last stages of Alzheimer's, he began to experience difficulty swallowing. Although he wanted to walk by himself and would try to, his legs would not hold him up, but getting him to stay in the wheelchair became contentious. Then he had a stroke. Decline was now the inevitable. How long did he have left? Two weeks? Two months? Longer? No one, however skilled, could answer that. The body, mind and heart set their own timetable.

Throughout this experience, I found myself contemplating the mystery that is life. Heartbeat, pulse, breath—yes, those are the physical signs that life is present. But do they represent life or merely existence? Surely they are not the same. What do we mean when we speak of life? Recognition? Yes, recognition of self, of the senses. Responsiveness? Yes, awareness of surroundings, taste, sensation, and touch and, above all, in the eyes, that light that says, "I am not just a body. I am a unique human being. I am a soul."

And I hoped that during these last days there would be the recognition that I too was a unique human being, a soul—that he would remember that I was the wife who loved him. If he could continue to give me that as we neared the end of our life together, I would feel truly blessed.

Death and Grieving

"THE REALITY IS YOU WILL GRIEVE FOREVER. YOU WILL NOT get over the loss of a loved one; you will learn to live with it. You will heal and you will rebuild yourself around the loss you have suffered. You will be whole again but you will never be the same again. Nor should you be, nor should you want to be."

Elizabeth Kubler-Ross

Good-bye, My Love

WHAT NANCY REAGAN CALLED "THE LONG GOOD-BYE" HAS, for us, come to an end.

My beloved husband died peacefully in his own home, surrounded by people who loved him.

It was indeed a long good-bye—seven years spent with Alzheimer's and a final year spent playing hide-and-seek with death.

We first felt death's presence a year before my husband died. It was a beautiful, brisk, bright January Saturday in Manhattan. We had lunch at our favourite French bistro, and although Alzheimer's had staked its claim, my husband was engaged with his surroundings—watching the many young families, smiling at the little girls, enjoying a Bloody Mary and a delicious lunch.

Outside, he said his back hurt, and then he told me he had to sit down. Almost instantly, he collapsed in my arms. Two men passing by noticed and moved to help me get him to a seat on a newspaper box, where he lost consciousness. They called an ambulance, and the verdict was a heart attack—followed by another heart attack in the emergency room and a week in the hospital.

He never really recovered from that experience. Once home, he seemed more confused and disoriented than before. Despite physical therapy, he never recaptured his balance or the strength in his legs. Whereas he had walked using a cane before, now he required a walker and then a wheelchair.

But the most serious consequence was a loss of courage on both our parts. The memory of him slipping away from me and losing consciousness in my arms was strong. Because of that and other more-practical reasons, going out with my husband became more difficult. He was sleeping almost 16 hours a day, so our life revolved around home. We began to live in an even narrower world.

Then death tapped on the door again. Breathing became more difficult—the diagnosis was congestive heart failure (CHF), and the verdict was that it was time for hospice. Although an outside observer might have looked at my husband's life and concluded that there wasn't much to live for, not much of what we think of as quality of life, clearly, he did not agree. Within three weeks, there was no longer a sign of CHF, and his breathing was normal. He failed the hospice test: he lived.

Death took a back seat, but Alzheimer's stepped up its pace, bringing more indignities to my gallant and elegant husband. Additional caregiving was required. Even so, we spent a summer at our home on Long Island, where we enjoyed the garden that was my husband's creation, visits from family and a long stay of two beloved Labrador retrievers, Clemmie and Luna, who, when they were not playing docile females to our King Charles cavalier, Brewster, monopolized the pool and then put large, wet heads on my husband's lap. It was a happy time—a never-to-be-forgotten two months of quiet joy.

Beside him, every day and every night, I did not notice the changes that were evident to those who did not see him so often.

He was losing ground both physically and mentally—he was weaker in the legs, needed a wheelchair more often and was less aware. Still, when we returned to New York and to the excellent care of the Irving Wright Center on Aging, part of the extraordinary New York Presbyterian Hospital, his vital signs were excellent, and there were signs of revival.

Around Christmas, there came some remarkable isolated moments when he was lucid and showed flashes of his old sense of humour. Those moments would catch us by surprise, and although fleeting and unconnected, they were precious.

I decided to go back out to Long Island over New Year's. I told him we were going, and he seemed to understand and to be looking forward to it. Our dear friend Dennis drove us out, and my husband, as always, sat in the front seat, where he and Dennis had more than once shared their assessments of the girls passing by.

Two days after New Year's, his speech was slurred. The next day, he had a small stroke. Local hospice was called in, and they advised me to suggest to the family that they come say good-bye. But by that afternoon, he was sitting up in bed, able to say to a visiting son and grandsons, "Thank you for coming to see me."

Had we dodged death once more? Later that day, he asked, "Where are we anchored?" and in the middle of the night, he insisted on sitting up and said, "I need to go to San Francisco." He never spoke again.

His breathing became so difficult that we brought in a hospital bed. I thought that might upset him, but by the time we moved him, he was in a coma. That night, alone in our bed, my beloved husband across the room in a hospital bed, was indescribable agony for me. That separation of a few feet felt like miles—a symbol of the eternal separation that was growing closer.

My children, his beloved stepchildren, arrived, along with a grandson and his wife. There was a constant rotation of people who loved him by his side, including our caregivers, Martha and Gene, and the caring nurses from Brookhaven Memorial Hospital Hospice. Our dog, perched on his back legs, would poke a nose through the rails to lick an inert hand.

One day, near the end of this vigil, my husband reached up, looked into my eyes, put his hand on my chin and turned my face away. What did that mean? Was he telling me to let him go? Perhaps. Two days later, six days after that small stroke, I was sitting by his bed with my son. It was midafternoon. I looked at him as he took a breath. I called out to the others, who rushed to the bedside. He was gone.

Wearing a pink silk pajama top, peacefully, quietly, he and his beautiful mind were serene and whole at last.

Death: Getting to Know You

Wᴇɴ ʏᴏᴜ ʀᴇᴀᴄʜ ᴀ ᴄᴇʀᴛᴀɪɴ ᴀɢᴇ, ʏᴏᴜ ꜱᴛᴀʀᴛ ᴛᴏ ʙᴇᴄᴏᴍᴇ familiar with death. Every year brings another round of funerals— so many that life can seem to be a long series of good-byes. When that reality becomes too sad, we have to remind ourselves of how glad we are that we had the hellos.

With each funeral, we realize two seemingly contradictory things: death is the universal experience, yet every death is unique.

In our minds, we categorize deaths. If you are a parent, the worst has to be the thought of the death of a child. The pain from that is unimaginable, but even so, we imagine it. And when it happens to the children of friends, we learn that the response to death is as unique as the dying. I have seen the death of a child bring a couple together in a way nothing else possibly could, and I have seen the different ways of mourning tear a husband and wife apart and, with it, their marriage.

When the daughter of a man I loved died in an automobile accident, all joy died with her. He could not allow himself to find delight in anything. "Every sunset," he said to me, "every piece of music, every good book, I think, she should be enjoying that, not me."

Yet a woman whose teenage son died of leukemia went on to absorb that loss and continue to live an engaged life. When I asked her how she survived, she said, "I am just very grateful for the years he was alive."

John Downing, a fellow Toronto journalist, shared with me a quote from Thornton Wilder regarding gratitude: "The highest tribute to the dead is not grief, but gratitude."

I understand that sentiment. I am grateful that my husband lived a long and productive life. I am grateful that I met him, that we fell in love, that we married and that we had many years together. I am grateful that he died before Alzheimer's inflicted even more indignities upon him. I am grateful that he died before I could no longer handle the caregiving and that I have no remorse. Above all, I am selfishly grateful that he died still recognizing me, that he remembered that I loved him, that he loved me and that those words were spoken.

The death that comes to an Alzheimer's patient whose self dies bit by bit long before the body does is different from the death that comes without warning, suddenly. The death that comes to someone elderly is different from the death that strikes down a young breadwinner. The death that is the end result of a long fight with pain is different from the death that steals a last breath while someone is peacefully sleeping. The death that comes from a violent act is like no other. All those left behind will mourn those deaths in different ways.

So please do not tell me how to grieve. I weep no tears because my husband has died. As our rabbi said, "Death came as a friend." It spared him more indignities. I do weep for the lost years. I weep for the younger family members who did not have the opportunity to truly know him. I weep for myself, for the silence of the house—how can it be so quiet, when it was never really noisy? I weep for the emptiness of the days that stretch before me without someone to care for. I weep for the uncertain future. I weep for the loosened ties. I am rudderless.

Do not tell me that you feel my pain, because you don't. None of us can feel another's pain. We can try. We can experience empathy. But we cannot truly feel another's pain. The skeins of life and emotions that are part of a person's grief and mourning are unique to that individual.

So do not assign me a stage as if the mysteries of the heart can be reduced to some cookie-cutter psychobabble. I will experience the coming days, weeks, and months in my own way, and I will work through them—or I won't—in my own clumsy fashion. If grief is still the dominant characteristic of my life after a year, then you might suggest that I see a grief counselor. I still might hit you. But I certainly will snap at you if you suggest such a thing now.

Who would I be—what kind of woman would I be—if I did not shed tears for someone I loved and lived with happily and joyously for 33 years? Leave me to my tears and to the healing that only tears can bring. Leave me to what is natural for anyone who has loved.

Spare me the euphemisms. My husband did not "pass." He died. I have not "lost" him—I know exactly where his body is, and his spirit is with me.

And do not speak to me of closure. What a hideous word—*closure*. If you have truly loved someone, you do not ever want to close off the memory of that love, the richness of that experience.

Let me be strong enough to absorb this death into my life, let it deepen my understanding of the mystery of life and let it make me wiser. Bring me acceptance but never closure.

Comforting the Widowed

THE DOCTOR RECORDS THE TIME AND DECLARES YOUR HUSBAND dead, and instantly, you are no longer a wife but a widow.

And you are thrust into all the arrangements that have to be made after a death, surrounded by people, moving one foot in front of the other through the public mourning, awash in paperwork and unimaginable questions, such as "How many death certificates will you need?"

When I wrote that I disliked euphemisms, such as *passed* or *lost* rather than *dead*, and that I could not bear the word *closure*, some readers thought that I was criticizing those individuals who might come to me and offer comfort using those words. That was not my intent. Tell me that you are sorry that I lost my husband or say how sad you were to hear that he passed, and I will say, "Thank you," and I will mean it. I will accept that this is the way you express your sympathy, and I will hear your words with my heart.

I was railing instead at a society that thinks of sadness and tears as aberrations that we should treat with pills or visits to a therapist, and a culture that cannot accept death as part of the cycle of life. Of course, most of us have trouble finding the right words to say to someone when a loved one dies. How could we not, when society uses words to deny the reality of the end of life?

How should we comfort the bereaved? Toronto writer Jane O'Hara reminded me of an interview Toni Morrison gave to Emma Brockes in the *Guardian*. Discussing the death of her son, Morrison said, "What do you say? There are really no words for that. There really aren't. Some people say, 'I'm sorry, I'm so sorry.' People say that to me. There's no language for it. Sorry doesn't do it. I think you should just hug people and mop their floor or something."

I can only say what works for me. What comforts me might alienate someone else. But I will take hugs—absolutely, I can't get enough of them—and practical help. You don't have to mop my floor, but please don't say, "Let me know if there is anything I can do," because I am never going to let you know. Or worse, don't say, "Call me if you need me." It is unlikely that I will ever make that call. But bring me a casserole sized for one. Drop off some bagels. Make sure I am eating, because I am not. That first stab at shopping for one, cooking for one, sitting at the table where he sat across from me for so many years, now by myself—I still haven't been able to do that, and the idea is so upsetting that I'd rather not eat. But if you drop by, bring a sandwich and sit with me, you will help me get over that hurdle.

I don't want to go to a noisy restaurant, to have to get dressed up. But invite me to your home with people who knew my husband, let me talk about him and make it casual and cozy. Don't be offended if I have to leave early. I am exhausted, and fatigue hits me suddenly like a moving train. Don't be offended if I make a date and then cancel. Don't be offended period.

Be the friend who volunteered to address the envelopes to the many letters I will now write. Offer to take the dog for a walk. Come watch *Downton Abbey* with me. Bring the Scotch. Tell me you are going shopping, and ask if I need anything. Help fill the silence of my life with a phone call, an offer to bring over a movie.

Be there when the others have gone, because most of the people who surrounded me in the first week are back at their own lives. I was touched by the delayed response of a friend who waited for three weeks to get in touch with me because she knew that by then, fewer people would be around.

Be patient with me. There will be days when I don't want to talk or see anyone, but the next day, I am restlessly searching for comfort. Do not be upset with me if I don't answer your call right away. I will in time. Don't be embarrassed if I cry. Don't get bored with my sorrow. My grief is not a two- or three-week wonder. It is unpredictable. A song, a bench, a man wearing a fedora—any of those things can make me suddenly cry. And my guess is that will go on for some time.

Above all, talk to me or write to me about my beloved. Make him live for me. Tell me how you knew him, what you learned from him and what you shared with him. We could have long debates about whether there is an afterlife or not and, if so, what form it would take. But we can surely agree that we all live on in the lives we touched on earth. Tell me how my husband's life touched yours.

Fortunately, I have received many letters like that, and they bring me joy. I read them with pleasure, often several times, and take my time with them, and I will answer them, each and every one, a few at a time, day after day and preserve them for family members to also read. Don't be afraid to tell me something funny about my husband. Humour was a great bond between us, and I love it when people share an amusing story about him. He would like to know that from beyond the grave, he is still able to make me smile.

Please do not disappear from my life. I know there are people who cannot deal with illness or death, because it reminds them of their own mortality. I feel sorry for them. They don't stay away because they are more sensitive than the rest of us—it is because they are afraid, and because of that fear, they cut themselves off from an important chapter of what makes us human. They have yet to learn that you can only truly experience life when you accept that death is part of it. Until then, you are living on the surface.

Others disappear because they don't know what to say. To that, I say this: Say anything, or say nothing. Bring a hug. Send an e-mail to ask, "How are you?"

Just be there. Your continuing presence in my life is the tribute you pay to my husband, to the history you shared with him; to our marriage and to the friendship I share with you. And words be damned, the friendship is what matters.

As to society and our culture, I will continue to rail in the hope that many other small voices might join my small voice to bring about a change, so that the day might come when we accept aging not as the new 50—what nonsense—but as the glory it is for itself. I long for a culture in which we enrich our every day, say what needs to be said and stand in awe at the wonder of our world all the more because we know our time on earth is limited.

Status:
The Alzheimer's Widow

Ten weeks have passed since my husband died—ten weeks of a new status: widow.

Widow—the word seems to beg to be followed by a period. Period. The end. The end of years of love, intimacy, sex, companionship, friendship, partnership and marriage. The end of a status: wife. Given that I spent the last seven years in the company of that thief Alzheimer's—years in which parts of my husband were gradually stolen from me day by day, week by week, month by month—one might wonder why the actual death is so painful.

I expected that I would feel relief—a burden lifted—but that has not happened. It is puzzling. Surely I have been saying good-bye for years, haven't I? Yes. But in those years, there was presence—the weight and sprawl of a body in bed, the sound of breathing, the touch of warm skin. With presence, there was possibility. Now there is absence and, with that, certainty. Period. The end.

In the beginning of this new status, I was numb. There was much to do—people to notify, a service to organize, others to comfort, paperwork to put in place, letters to answer. And then there was exhaustion, a deep, years-old fatigue of body and spirit—the sum of years of sleeping yet not quite sleeping. Now I slept—and slept.

Awake, I did not know what to do with my days. I was unmoored, lost. I wanted to be alone. I wanted company. I made appointments and then cancelled them, started something and then left it undone and wandered through the apartment, marvelling at how noisy silence can be. I never understood why people would turn on the television and leave it on when they were not watching it. Now that nonsensical murmur is my companion too.

I set grief aside, but it was there, clamoring to be let out. It came in many guises—terrible restlessness that made me want to run, unfocussed anger, lack of patience with nonsense—and to my surprise, it assumed physical form, including nausea and attacks of hyperventilation. The tears were beating against my skin—constant and contained but there.

I comfort myself with things. While walking the dog, I wear my husband's scarf and gloves. I sleep in his nightshirt and wrap myself in his cardigan when there is a chill. I touch his ties, shirts and jackets. I savour the remnants of Eau Sauvage and turn my head at the smell of a cigar—to the cigar, not from it. I consider the last bottle of wine he ordered and can't bring myself to drink it.

People reach out, and I appreciate that. I want to talk about my husband, hear stories about him, know what he meant to others and especially share anecdotes that have, at their heart, laughter. There has also been an onslaught of advice: Move. Don't move. Go back to Toronto. Stay in New York. Do something. Do nothing. Don't throw anything away. Call in the Salvation Army and get rid of everything. My favourite was a suggestion that I wear more rouge. The yuckiest was which online dating service to employ. Please!

People tell me I am lucky—lucky to have known such a love and lucky to have such glorious memories. Yes, that's true, but that is also the source of the pain. The greater the love, the greater the sorrow. People tell me that life goes on, and yes, I know that. That is why I weep. I sit in the park with our dog, and I see life going on all around me. How can that be? Should the world not stop when such a splendid human being dies?

There has also been a plethora of articles and books on how to grieve. What, I wonder, did previous generations do without all these how-to manuals? Has all this instruction made us better lovers, parents and managers of money, crises, and our planet than our parents were? Is there any part of life today that has not been commercialized and turned into a get-rich how-to formula for someone?

Fortunately, all the advice on grieving and mourning comes to the same conclusion: each person has to find his or her own way. I am glad of that. My marriage was mine, unique to me. I want to own my own mourning too, thank you very much, not have it reduced to a common denominator.

This week, number 10 of being a widow, will also mark what I suspect is the first of a year of terrible firsts, including a 33rd anniversary with no husband to raise a glass to me, to ask, as he did every year, "Joan, would you do it over again?"

Yes, my darling. I would do it all again, even the last years—in a minute. But for now, I relive it. When I see a good-looking man tip his hat to a woman, automatically assuming that she is a lady, I smile. And I cry—at the same time. That is how I mourn.

Grief: The Poor-Me Stage

BY NOW, MOST PEOPLE RECOGNIZE THAT THE STAGES OF GRIEF adopted from the Kübler-Ross model of the stages of death are not a map. Each of us walks that lonely road in our own way. Still, when anger, restlessness or loneliness overcomes you, it is helpful to know that others have been down this path and have managed to reach places of healing.

But there is one aspect of grief that no one talks about it, because it isn't considered "nice." Listings of the stages don't mention it. It's not ennobling, and it's not romantic—it's just unattractive. In this world where words are so often used to cloak the truth (people don't lie anymore—they just "misspeak"), the tendency would be to soften what I am about to say.

But let's be blunt and admit it: some part of grief is just plain feeling sorry for oneself.

Yes, I miss my husband terribly, and I mourn his absence. However, within that sorrow, there is also an element of self-pity, which has its irony, because during the seven years I was a caregiver, I completely rejected any thought that anyone should feel sorry for me. I would say, "It looks worse from the outside than it actually is." And it did. Or I'd say, "I am where I want to be, doing what I want to do—there is no need to pity me."

I did not feel sorry for myself. There was a purpose to my days; I was responding to a real need. I was doing my duty and bringing love to it. And I was getting lots back—sometimes from my husband and often from others. But now? There are moments when I have to admit that I am just wallowing in poor-Joan mode.

Why? Because I have to make serious, painful decisions by myself. That seems ridiculous on the surface because I have been making those decisions for the last seven years without any poor-me thoughts. What's the difference?

Well, then there was hope. However improbable and impossible I knew it to be, as long as my husband was alive, there was a chance someone would create the magic pill—a chance that suddenly, miraculously, he would be back to take charge. Death not only took my husband but also stole that hope. I am now alone, and the decisions are mine alone to make. That is a fact that I can't duck, deny or avoid.

Death is the great clarifier. It brings us face to face with all the elements that we took for granted in our lives. I am a sensual human being, and I took intimacy for granted. Helping my husband bathe was the last aspect of caregiving I gave up—and only then because I could not safely manage it. Right to the end, until his last breath, I touched my husband—felt skin on skin, embraced him and kissed him. Now I must face the fact that at the age of 80, it is highly unlikely I will ever know that kind of intimacy again. I suffer from what I can only call skin hunger—grievous loss upon grievous loss.

During those seven years, although I did not have someone I could talk to, I did have someone I could talk at, and the talking helped me sort out problems and make decisions. Now I talk both to and at my dog, and he is an excellent listener. His head tips to the side; he looks right into my eyes with a serious, worried expression; and he doesn't interrupt. But he misses his master as much as I do and he can only snuggle up to my husband's pillow, looking for the answers there.

Many of you will suggest that I consult a therapist, but it's hard to believe that someone who doesn't know me can help me decide what to do with the rest of my life. And my Scottish soul resists the thought of actually paying someone to listen to me. How humiliating is that! Group discussions tend to depress me even more: I go in sad and come out desperate. It does not help to know that there is not just my grief but also a world of grief out there—my misery does not love that much company.

I could talk to friends, but many of them have time limits about mourning—"Seven months and you are not over it?" Those who are willing to listen also tend to give advice, which they expect you to follow. And if you don't, they are likely to throw up their hands and give up on you. Many people—excuse me for stereotyping, but especially men—don't want to discuss the problem. They want to give you the solution. Period. Done. That is that.

It's also lonelier now. My loneliness has its basis in more than my husband's absence. During the last phase of the caregiving, there were two others sharing the vigil. We were a team, discussing the day with each other, giving each other encouragement and helping each other through the bad moments. The visiting nurse came and went, and the geriatric staff and then the nurturing hospice staff checked in. They checked on the patient, and they checked on me. All that bustle, consultation and daily sharing of concerns is finished, and in its stead, there is a home that is unbearably quiet and still.

I haven't been abandoned; friends do invite me out. Although I've always had a certain poise and making an entrance has never thrown me, now I can't take walking into large gatherings by myself. I prefer being with one or two people for a quiet evening of conversation. But the warmth of such gatherings just magnifies the emptiness I feel when I return home. The contrast is too sharp. I go out to ease the loneliness, only to find that it waits behind the door, quick to remind me that absence is the presence in our home.

Most people who find themselves in the world of widows and widowers—men as well as women—also face practical lifestyle adjustments, many of them financial. If there was a pension, it might suddenly be less; the costs of additional caregivers will have eroded savings. Even if a move isn't financially necessary, the house or apartment might now be too big or too full of painful memories. How does one manage? How does one move on? How can one build a new life when one is still longing for the old?

It's enough to make you feel sorry for yourself—and most of us do.

The Mind-and-Body
Connection

IT TOOK SOME OF THE MEDICAL ESTABLISHMENT A LONG TIME
to recognize the mind-and-body connection—which is surprising
when you consider that connection is an integral part of our
vocabulary.

When children are overactive, a mother scolds, "Be still—you
are giving me a headache." When we are angry with someone, we
say we are going to give him or her an earful or the back of our
hand. If the person answers back, he or she is mouthy or gives us lip.
Vengeful, we want to stick our finger in someone's eye. Sedated, we
are glassy-eyed; determined, we are steely-eyed; romantic, we are
dewy-eyed; and out of our minds, we are wild-eyed. A pretty girl
is an eyeful. Someone who is intrusive is nosy; a fancy word or an
ill-considered judgment is a mouthful. Taste applies to more than
food, and to find something distasteful is to say it all.

When asked to do something that offends us, we reply we don't
have the stomach for it. We might make decisions based on gut
feelings. We give someone a shoulder to cry on, a helping hand or a

leg up. When we make a mistake or say something impolite, we put our foot in our mouth. We call a bratty child or a difficult partner a handful. Stymied, we throw up our hands. We tell people to get off our back, that they are a pain in the neck and, sometimes, a pain in the ass. When encouraging someone to be brave, we suggest he or she keep the chin up or show some spine.

If you act without thinking, you lose your head. When you fall in love, you do so head over heels. When we provide an introduction to someone seeking a job, we have given him or her a foot or a toe in the door. A dishonourable man is a heel. The genitals are metaphors for manliness and softness. When we want refuge, we go back to the womb. Used as an adjective, the heart lends definition to a meal or a laugh.

The brain might be the intellectual centre of our body, but while the brain is still sifting facts, I might simply do what my heart says is right. The poets and songwriters agree: the heart knows. What we ascribe to the heart has no relation to what the heart is: a well-constructed but not very pretty utilitarian pump—not vastly different from pumps we use in our everyday lives. But no other pump is described the way the heart is. The heart feels. In the words of a song that, in its original form, dates back to Marie Antoinette, "It cries for you, sighs for you, dies for you."[13]

The heart can be wounded; it aches. It can be heavy with sorrow, be sick with worry, leap for joy and burst with happiness. It is mobile; far from diligently pumping away in your chest, it might be anywhere—on your sleeve, in your mouth, in your hand, dropped to the floor or in your stomach. You can give your heart away, and if you are not careful, you might lose it.

---

13   Percy Faith and Carl Sigman, "My Heart Cries for You" (New York: Lyrics Universal Music Publishing Group, 1950).

The heart has texture: yours might be hard or soft, tender or so impermeable we cry out, "Have you no heart?" The pump continues to pump in people who are thought of as heartless. It can be expansive: "I will hold you in my heart." It can be a jail: "I will keep you in my heart." Or it can be used in punishment: "I will lock you out of my heart." The heart, they tell us, has its reasons. It makes judgments: "My heart tells me this is just a fling."[14]

It is responsive: faced with something unusual, it might race or it might stop. It will certainly pound. When one heart meets another heart, the two can beat as one—perhaps even in three-quarter time.

And when those two hearts have become entwined—when they learn to beat as one, when they are leaping with joy and bursting with happiness—along comes death.

Death reaches out and stills but one of the beating hearts, leaving the other to pulse alone.

What then? "None but the lonely heart / Can know my sorrow."[15]

And what the lonely hearts know is this: Hearts can—and do—break.

I know.

---

14   Harry Warren and Mack Gordon, "My Heart Tells Me This Is Just a Fling" (Lyrics@Warner/Chappell Music, Inc., 1943).

15   Pytor Ilyich Tchaikovsky and Johann Wolfgang von Goethe, "None but the Lonely Heart," 1869.

The If-Onlys

MY HUSBAND USED TO JOKE ABOUT HOW HE WOULD PREFER to die—after a martini, a great dinner with good friends and a fabulous bottle of wine, followed by a Cuban cigar, an Armagnac, passionate lovemaking and a deep sleep from which he would not wake up.

Well, he did all those things, except the last, many times. To my joy, he always woke up.

He was equally adamant about how he did not want to die and repeatedly said, "If I get Alzheimer's, take me out and shoot me."

Well, he did get Alzheimer's, and I did not shoot him, nor did he shoot himself. Did he know? Here we come to the big ifs. If he did know, in time, would he have followed through on his determination to end his life rather than suffer the indignities of Alzheimer's?

It's a rhetorical question, because he did not know, and neither did I. Looking back, in retrospect, I can see that the signs were there, but we missed them; we dismissed them as the result of hearing loss, information overload, stress, fatigue or just getting older. That is one of the many problems of trying to diagnose

AD early on: at its outset, it can be an incremental disease, with symptoms that might be placed at many doors. By the time we finally went to a neurologist, my husband was no longer capable of making any decisions, let alone one to end his life.

We had both signed living wills, and with every medical advance, we'd amended them, becoming more and more specific about what we did not want to have done to us. But the living will is an intellectual exercise, most often written when none of those things are imminent, suspected or known. We were healthy, strong and active, and we did not anticipate that anyone would have to act on those directives soon. And although our living wills specified that in the event we experienced "a mental state from which there was no reasonable expectation of recovery, our lives should not be prolonged," there was no clause to deal with AD itself. AD is not a disease that calls for life-sustaining treatments; there is no machine to stop, no button labelled "End Indignity" to turn off.

Not only did I not shoot my husband, but given the opportunity to perhaps shorten his time, I could not do it. He had a heart attack. He was an elderly man in the grips of Alzheimer's, needing constant care. An intervention made no sense. I had his power of attorney, his health-care proxy and a copy of the directives in my hand. But the cardiologist's job is saving hearts, and I heard so many reasons why this intervention would be a good thing that I gave in to the pressure and permitted the surgery.

My guess is that surgery added a year to my husband's life, but it did not add any life to that year. Quite the opposite—his last year was the worst. Perhaps it would have been anyway—some things we cannot know. As for my husband, when the brain no longer controlled his decisions, his body took command.

When the intellect dies, the body speaks. The brain demands quality of life. The body does not care about quality; it just wants to go on living no matter what. Therefore, for seven years, we battled daily with AD, and there wasn't a day when I didn't think of how my husband had said he wanted to die and lament the reality. I took solace in the sad knowledge that he did not seem to know what had happened to him; those who loved him saw the loss of self, the erosion of the man we knew, but except on rare occasions, he did not seem to mind. He was not in pain, he was well cared for and he appeared to be comfortable, even—so long as we kept to a rigid schedule—content.

Ah, the if-onlys. If only we had known, what would we have done?

I like to think that we were already living life as it should be lived—valuing what mattered, making sure those we loved knew they were loved, making the most of every day and appreciating the beauty of the woods, our garden and birdsong.

It is easy to rewrite the past, but I think that had we known, we would have organized one more magical moment with family and friends—a time made richer by the knowledge of what was ahead— and then we might have taken a last trip together, visiting old haunts, walking in our own footsteps and celebrating our love. At the end of that trip, I would have suggested that we move to Washington or Oregon, where Death with Dignity Acts are in place—not only legal but also, under the right circumstances, accessible. So we could take that last step together. I was ready, more than ready, to die with him.

Get out the violins. That is a misty, gauze-covered view of what might have been. It leaves out all the messy stuff—the cold-eyed decision, the preparations, the consultations with family, the actual doing of the final act—which is why, perhaps, despite the access to a death with dignity, few seem to actually take advantage of the law. In the 15 years since the law was passed in Oregon, 935 people—citing decreasing ability to participate in activities that made life enjoyable, loss of autonomy and loss of dignity as reasons—had Death with Dignity Act prescriptions written. Of those, only 596 actually took the prescriptions. In Washington State, 103 prescriptions were issued in one year, and 70 actually took the medication.

The living will and the will to live: two concepts apparently sometimes at odds.

The Not-So-Merry Widow

I AM MOVING THROUGH WHAT I THINK OF AS THE YEAR OF terrible firsts without him: the first wedding anniversary, the first holidays, the first family wedding and the first birthdays—his, mine and our children's.

And I move inexorably to the marking of the first anniversary of his death.

In many ways, these months have been full of surprises.

Who would have thought I would miss caregiving? But I do. Apparently, it is addictive. I miss being needed, being useful and having someone to look after. When I am sure that I am emotionally stable enough to be a dependable volunteer, I will fill that need by volunteering. But in the meantime, my days are without purpose. I am rootless. As a caregiver, I didn't go to the theatre, because I didn't want to be away from a telephone for that long. Now I could go to the theatre every day, and I haven't been once.

Who would have thought that silence could be so intrusive? Coming home to the empty, much-too-quiet apartment is painful. When observing other widows and widowers, I see a tendency to be anywhere but home. They just keep moving—taking trips, going on cruises and busying themselves, it seems to me, with busyness. I can only assume that being constantly on the move must delay, if not ease, the pain of absence.

Travelling might be a solution, but I don't have the energy for it, and I am so restless that although I might think I want to go somewhere else, when I get there, I don't want to be there either. Everything is an effort. The seven years I spent caregiving have taken their toll. I am exhausted. Add to that the deep sadness, the new responsibilities, the decisions I must make and the changes, real or contemplated, and I quickly use what energy I have. I might make plans, but I soon run out of steam.

Who would have thought that one could hoard tears? But I think that is what I am doing. Yes, I cried when my husband died and for a few days between his death and funeral. But since then, despite being sometimes overwhelmed with grief, the tears do not come. They are inside, pulsing against my skin. I wonder if I hold them back because I am fearful that if I let them out, my memory of my husband will dissipate with them?

I acknowledge that I am holding on fiercely to my mourning. I don't want to "get over it." I am not sure what people mean when they use that phrase. Is my husband's death like a hurdle, a fence that I must climb over? I should get over what? Loving my husband? Missing him? The other common advice involves "moving on." Again, what does that mean? Where, to what condition, to what state do I move? If I move on, do I leave behind what went before?

The truth is that I don't want to get over it. Indeed, I think a psychiatrist or psychologist would look at the absence of my tears over the past 11 months and conclude that I am putting off mourning, holding on to my husband by refusing to weep for him. In a way, the unshed tears hold him close; they make it possible for me to deny the reality of his death.

Nor do I want to move on—not if that means forgetting. The thought that I might forget my husband, forget our years together, is appalling. Getting over it, moving on—these phrases sound like disloyalty to my husband, a kind of infidelity.

Kind friends tell me that my husband would want me to move on. Perhaps, although I wonder how they know. But I didn't always do what he wanted me to do when he was alive, and I'm not sure I want to do so now.

More than that, I think that if I am to heal, I need to walk right into the middle of this pain—to accept it, understand it and learn to live with it. I take great comfort in this quote from Elizabeth Kübler-Ross:

> The reality is you will grieve forever. You will not get over the loss of a loved one; you will learn to live with it. You will heal and you will rebuild yourself around the loss you have suffered. You will be whole again but you will never be the same again. Nor should you be, nor should you want to be.

Anima

LIVING WITH ALZHEIMER'S IS A LESSON IN THE MYSTERY OF life.

Pieces of self just disappear.
Good-bye, husband, head of the household.
Good-bye, husband, chief gardener.
Good-bye, husband, master chef.
Good-bye, husband, protector, friend, confidant.
Good-bye to the man who told me I was lovely.
Good-bye, good-bye, good-bye.

The voracious maw of Alzheimer's swallows fragments of self bit by bit. So many pieces flew away over the years that I found myself wondering, *What is self? Which aspects of it are essential? What makes us human? What is left when self disappears?* Consider the eyes. One day, they are vibrant. They not only see but also reveal—they mirror. They are eloquent. Look away, and when you look back, in what seems a mere second, the mirror is blank. The eyes are there, and they function. They see, but there is nothing to see in them. They are vacant. Many writers have expressed the thought that the eyes are the mirror of the soul. If that is so, when the eyes go dead, does that mean the soul has died before the man?

As my husband and I descended deeper into the abyss of Alzheimer's, I found myself thinking more and more of the Latin word *anima*, which suggests to me the life force, the difference between being human or merely a shell. Some call it the soul or spirit, but *anima* resonates with me because my husband was always animated—he had a big, warm smile, eyes alight with interest, humour, tenderness and a body always in motion.

I could describe my husband by telling you his height and weight and outlining the perfectly shaped head, the long back, the narrow feet and the beautiful hands. I could do that so well that you could picture him. But you would not see him—unless you could also conjure up the anima.

When you are with someone when he or she dies, you become acutely aware of that life force, because suddenly, with one breath not taken, it is gone, and the difference is both profound and devastating. On the threshold of death, you vividly see the true meaning of life. Over the Alzheimer's years, I lamented the loss of my husband's abilities and strengths, but those losses were suddenly irrelevant, just tiny chips in the identity of the man—nothing compared to death itself.

I was at my husband's side. He had been in a coma for several days, but life was still there. He was still with us. There was breath, colour in the skin, warmth in the hand and a reflexive twitch that might have been—could have been (please!)—recognition. Then, in an instant, all that changed. I am still shocked at how quick the transition was—one breath not taken, and colour, warmth and anima left the body immediately.

My husband was gone. I saw him go one year ago today. The body remained, and it was as handsome, elegant and distinguished as ever. A few days later, we would bury that body according to the solemn rituals of his religion.

But his body was not what I loved. I loved the invisible, indescribable self.

Call it soul, spirit, anima—that is what sets us apart and gives meaning to existence.

The elegant man—my dancing, life-loving partner—is buried. But the anima remains. It lives on, as the rabbis say, in the lives he touched on earth and in the hearts of those who loved him. And in yet another reflection of the mystery of life, it lives on in a more palpable, intimate way: as a vibrant presence—invisible and inexplicable but real—beside me and surrounding me at unexpected times.

I am, by choice, spending today alone—no phone calls, no e-mail exchanges, and no company. The memorial candle is lit; the skies are grey. I will listen to music we shared together, revisit our life in photographs and allow myself to be open to the anima.

He, my beloved, is—and will be—with me.

The Widow's Dower:
Skin Hunger

Fifteen months into widowhood, what do I miss?
Touch. Talk.

Sex, yes, of course, but the desire for that pales beside the need to be touched. I have a serious case of skin hunger.

Couples who live together in intimacy take for granted the many times in a day when they touch each other, from bumping into one another in the bathroom to fingertips brushing over a coffee cup or one cold foot seeking out the warmer one under the blanket.

I miss my husband's hands on my back, applying the suntan lotion in the hard-to-reach place; moving up and down with the zipper, turning my shoulders to the light where, his face a picture of fierce concentration, he would try to fasten a clasp on a necklace or that tiny hook at the top of the dress, swearing all the while. Then, when he had conquered that pesky closing, he would plant a kiss on the nape of my neck.

I miss his hip touching mine in the backseat of a taxi, his hand under my elbow when we cross a street, the pressure on my arm, holding me back when I don't see a car coming.

I miss that hand gently tucking an errant hair back behind my ear; at the back of my neck, pulling me into an embrace; two fingers pressed against my lips in a symbolic kiss or as a way of telling me to stop talking, that my worries are foolish. I miss the way he wrapped his arms around me in a hug, when he held my coat for me, the playful pat on the bottom in the kitchen; the hand grasping mine at a poignant moment in a film. I miss him pulling me into his arms to dance, feeling his body lead mine, one hand on my waist, our legs moving together in rhythm.

I miss his touch—on my forehead, checking to see if I have a fever, kneading a sore muscle—his hands, applying the Band-Aid, holding out the water and the aspirin.

I remember now that when he came to the dining table, before he sat down, he would just brush my shoulder. I hardly noticed it at the time. But was more than a touch, it was his way of saying "The food smells good, the table looks pretty, I am glad to be here with you." All that, communicated with the smallest stroke. Which I took for granted.

And it is that kind of talk that I miss, the kind that doesn't need words. The mutual irritation we would feel when some blowhard sucked all the energy out of the room and took over the conversation at the dinner party; the way, without a word or even looking at each other, we knew it was time to leave the cocktail party, turn off the uncivil television talk show, the moment to move into the shade, to have a drink, to go to bed.

I miss the verbal kind of talk too, the analysis at the end of the evening of what went before and above all, the safety in the security that, whatever we said, would not be repeated or held against us and that, next morning, we could recant. But that kind of conversation disappeared from our marriage a very long time ago, swallowed up by that thief, Alzheimer's.

So, from this sad place of widowdom, let me urge those of you who have loving, living partners, to cherish and acknowledge the insignificant, uncounted, taken for granted, touch and talk aspect of your life together.

Those are the things to treasure; they are what, should life be interrupted, you will surely miss.

Endless Love

I HAVE TO REMIND MYSELF THAT OUR LOVE DID not always exist.

Somehow I lived without it. I was content in my acceptance that this would be life: children, cat, dog, friends, work—a lot—but not love.

But love began. It started as a flame and then expanded, enveloped, became an integral part of my life, woven into my days and nights.

How quickly we take things for granted. How foolish.

Death came, and life was interrupted.

But not love.

Love is more powerful than life.

What once did not exist now has no end.

What began as an emotional strike of lightning

Is now a perfect circle,

Not dependent on breath, life, presence.

It just is.

Forever.

Love.

I loved.

And I was loved.

How I was loved.

Lucky me,

To have known you,

To have been known by you.

Lucky, lucky me.

Bibliography

Every public library contains a vast assortment of books that deal with aspects of caregiving, Alzheimer's and other forms of dementia. This list contains only the material that I found personally to be useful.

"A Conversation with Senator Susan Collins." *AARP Bulletin* (December 2013): 8–9.

"Alzheimer's Disease Progress Report." National Institutes of Health, National Institute on Aging, Alzheimer's Disease Education and Referral Center (2012–13).

Brockes, Emma. "Interview with Toni Morrison." *Guardian*, April 13, 2012.

Faith, Percy, and Carl Sigman. "My Heart Cries for You." Universal Music Publishing Group, 1950.

Fillit, Howard, MD, and R. N. Butler, MD. *Cognitive Decline: Strategies for Prevention* (London: Greenwich Medical Media, 1997).

Gross, Jane. *A Bittersweet Season, Caring for Our Aging Parents* (New York: Vintage, 2012).

Innes, K.E., T. K. Self, C. J. Browne, K. M. Rose, and A. Thomson Heisterman. "The Effect of Meditation on Perceived Stress and Related Indices of Psychological States and Sympathetic Activation in Persons with Alzheimer's Disease and Their Caregivers: A Pilot Study," *Evidence Based Complementary and Alternative Medicine*, Volume 2012.

Mace, Nancy L., MA, and Peter V. Rabins, MD, MPH. *The 36-Hour Day. A Family Guide to Caring for People Who Have Alzheimer's Disease, Related Dementias, and Memory Loss* (Baltimore: Johns Hopkins University Press, 2011).

McCullough, Dennis, MD. *My Mother, Your Mother What to Expect When Parents Age.* (Boston: Harper Collins, 2009).

Shakespeare, William. *As You Like It.* Act 2, Scene 7.

Sheehy, Gail. *Passages in Caregiving Turning Chaos Into Confidence.* (New York: William Morrow, 2010).

Tchaikovsky, Pyotr Ilyich. "None but the Lonely Heart." Lyrics by Johann Wolfgang von Goethe, 1869.

Warren, Harry, and Gordon Mack. "My Heart Tells Me This Is Just a Fling." (Lyrics@Warner/Chappell Music, Inc., 1943).

Westheimer, Ruth K., MD, (author) and Pierre A. Lehu (contributor). *Dr. Ruth's Guide for the Alzheimer Caregiver.* (Fresno, California: Quill Driver Books, 2012).

Wilder, Thornton. *The Bridge of San Luis Rey* (New York: Albert and Charles Boni, 1927).